Mastering Concurrent Programming in Go
A Comprehensive Guide

Adam Jones

Contents

Preface

The rapid evolution of computer hardware, coupled with the relentless increase in available processing power, has elevated concurrent programming to a pivotal role in modern software development. Today's applications—ranging from web servers and cloud services to complex distributed systems—depend heavily on concurrent execution mechanisms to optimize efficiency and enhance performance. The Go programming language, renowned for its groundbreaking approach to concurrency, stands as a premier choice for developers eager to leverage the full potential of contemporary multicore and networked systems.

This book, *Mastering Concurrent Programming in Go: A Comprehensive Guide*, is meticulously crafted to equip developers with the proficiency required to master Go's sophisticated concurrency constructs. It provides an in-depth exploration of the concurrency model that underpins Go, covering essential elements such as goroutines, channels, and the sync package. The book further delves into intricate topics, including pattern-based concurrency, performance optimization, and troubleshooting concurrency-related issues.

Our structured approach ensures a seamless progression from foundational principles to complex applications, enabling readers to build on their understanding incrementally. Beginning with a comprehensive introduction to the essence of concurrency and the strategic design choices made by Go to facilitate robust concurrent programming, we then transition to more intricate details. Readers will gain a thorough grasp of goroutines, the cornerstone of concurrency in Go, and channels, which serve as the primary mechanism for inter-goroutine communication. Following this, we delve into synchronization primitives, explore advanced channel patterns, and unveil concurrent design patterns alongside best practices for concurrency safety.

Significant emphasis is placed on the practical application of these concepts, illustrated through numerous examples and case studies inspired by real-world scenarios. Additionally, we address the inherent challenges posed by concurrent programming, such as race conditions, deadlock, and livelock. We present strategies for their identification, prevention, and resolution to foster the development of safe and efficient concurrent applications.

Designed for intermediate to advanced Go developers, *Mastering Concurrent Programming in Go: A Comprehensive Guide* assumes a working familiarity with Go's basic syntax and concepts. It is an invaluable resource for software developers intent on deepening their understanding of concurrency to bolster the performance, efficiency, and scalability of their Go applications. Moreover, it offers seasoned Go programmers a comprehensive reference to refine their skills, explore novel patterns, and adopt best practices in concurrent programming.

By the conclusion of this book, readers will have acquired a comprehensive understanding of Go's concurrency model and its application in crafting robust, efficient, and secure concurrent applications. Armed with this expertise, developers will be well-equipped to tackle the intricate challenges of contemporary software development, maximizing the concurrency capabilities offered by Go to drive innovation and impact.

Chapter 1

Introduction to Concurrency in Go

Concurrency is a fundamental aspect of modern software development, allowing programs to perform multiple operations simultaneously to enhance performance and efficiency. Go, a statically typed programming language developed by Google, offers built-in support for concurrency, making it an appealing choice for developers working on high-performance and scalable applications. This chapter introduces the basic concepts of concurrency in Go, including its distinction from parallelism, the role of goroutines and channels, and how these elements fit into Go's concurrency model. Through understanding these foundational concepts, developers can begin to leverage Go's capabilities to build more responsive and efficient applications.

1.1 What is Concurrency?

Concurrency is a concept that, at its core, revolves around making progress on more than one task simultaneously. It is pivotal in the development of efficient and high-performance software applications. In the domain of computing, concurrency is a technique whereby multiple tasks are in progress at the same time but do not necessarily have to be executed simultaneously. This approach can vastly improve the responsiveness and throughput of a software system.

In the Go programming language, designed by Google, concurrency is a fundamental principle that is baked into the language itself, offering a robust set of features to handle concurrent operations gracefully. Go's concurrency is predicated on the Communicating Sequential Processes (CSP) model, which facilitates concurrent execution through the use of goroutines and channels.

Goroutines are lightweight threads of execution managed by the Go runtime. They are less resource-intensive than traditional threads, making it feasible to create thousands, even millions, of goroutines in a single application. Here's a simple illustration of creating a goroutine in Go:

```
1   package main
2
3   import (
4       "fmt"
5       "time"
6   )
7
8   func sayHello() {
9       fmt.Println("Hello, world!")
10  }
11
12  func main() {
13      go sayHello()
14      time.Sleep(1 * time.Second)
15  }
```

In this example, the sayHello function is executed in a separate goroutine. The time.Sleep call is there to ensure that the main goroutine does not exit before sayHello is executed since the Go runtime does not wait for other goroutines to finish execution once the main goroutine completes.

Channels, on the other hand, are Go's way of allowing goroutines to communicate with each other, ensuring synchronization without the explicit use of locks or conditional variables typically seen in other programming languages. Here's how you might create and use a simple channel:

```
1   package main
2
3   import "fmt"
4
5   func main() {
6       messages := make(chan string)
7
8       go func() { messages <- "ping" }()
9
10      msg := <-messages
11      fmt.Println(msg)
12  }
```

In the above snippet, a channel named messages is created. A goroutine is then spawned that sends a string "ping" to this channel. The main goroutine waits to receive a message from the messages channel and prints it upon reception. The execution of these operations is concurrent, demonstrating a basic inter-goroutine communication pattern.

Concurrency in Go is not a mere tool but a fundamental aspect of the language's design philosophy. With goroutines and channels, Go simplifies the task of writing reliable, concurrent programs, making concurrency a first-class citizen in the language's ecosystem. This design choice reflects in the ease with which developers can architect systems that are highly responsive and efficient, achieving concurrency without the complexity traditionally associated with multithreaded programming.

1.2 Concurrency vs. Parallelism

In this section, we will discuss the distinction between concurrency and parallelism, both of which are crucial concepts in the world of programming, specifically when dealing with high-performance computing. While often used interchangeably in casual conversation, these terms have distinct meanings and implications in the context of programming with Go.

Concurrency refers to the ability of a program to manage multiple tasks at the same time. It is more about the structure of a program and the way it is conceptualized to handle multiple tasks. For instance, a concurrent program could be designed to handle user input, perform calculations, and update the UI simultaneously. The key idea is that the program is structured in such a way that it can deal with many tasks by executing them out of order or in any order without affecting the final outcome.

Parallelism, on the other hand, describes the scenario where tasks are literally running at the same time, exploiting the capabilities of multi-core processors. In essence, parallelism requires concurrency as a foundation but takes it a step further by executing multiple operations simultaneously. This is particularly beneficial when performing computationally heavy operations that can be divided into smaller, independent tasks and run simultaneously to improve performance.

An important concept to grasp here is that while all parallelism is a form of concurrency, not all concurrency is parallelism. This distinction is crucial in understanding how Go approaches the management of multiple tasks. Below is a simplified code example that demonstrates concurrency in Go using goroutines, not to be confused with parallel execution but as a foundation for achieving parallelism.

```
 1  package main
 2
 3  import (
 4    "fmt"
 5    "time"
 6  )
 7
 8  func main() {
 9    go count("sheep")
10    count("fish")
11  }
12
13  func count(thing string) {
14    for i := 1; i <= 5; i++ {
15      fmt.Println(i, thing)
16      time.Sleep(time.Millisecond * 500)
17    }
18  }
```

In the above example, the count function is called in two different contexts: once normally, and once as a goroutine (using the go keyword). This demonstrates concurrency as the Go runtime makes no guarantees about which go routine executes first or whether they run in parallel. The scheduling and execution are managed internally and can vary. To verify the concurrent nature of this setup, observe the interleaved output that demonstrates the concurrent execution.

```
1 sheep
1 fish
2 sheep
2 fish
3 sheep
3 fish
4 sheep
4 fish
5 sheep
5 fish
```

From an academic perspective, understanding the distinction between concurrency and parallelism in Go is pivotal. Concurrency in Go allows developers to structure applications that can efficiently manage multiple tasks, potentially exploiting the underlying hardware to achieve parallel execution where appropriate. However, Go's runtime scheduler plays a critical role in how these concurrent tasks are executed, potentially allowing for parallelism based on the program's design and the available computing resources.

Through this lens, it becomes apparent that concurrency in Go is a foundational building block towards achieving parallelism. Developers can leverage goroutines to develop highly concurrent applications, and with careful structuring and understanding of Go's scheduling and runtime, those applications can often realize significant performance benefits through parallel execution.

1.3 The Evolution of Concurrency in Go

The design and implementation of concurrency in Go has been significantly shaped by its predecessors and the requirements of modern computing. The inception of Go's concurrency model is deeply rooted in the concept of Communicating Sequential Processes (CSP), a formal language for describing patterns of interaction in concurrent systems, introduced by Tony Hoare in 1978. CSP's influence on Go is apparent in the language's emphasis on message passing as the primary means of communication between concurrent processes, or goroutines in Go's terminology.

The evolution of concurrency in Go can be traced back to its initial release in 2009. From the outset, Go was designed to address the complexities of concurrent programming encountered in large-scale system development at Google. The language's creators, Robert Griesemer, Rob Pike, and Ken Thompson, aimed to develop a programming language that facilitated efficient parallel execution of processes while maintaining simplicity and readability.

- **Inception**: In the early versions, Go introduced goroutines as a lightweight thread managed by the Go runtime scheduler. Unlike traditional threads, goroutines require significantly less memory overhead, allowing thousands of them to be spawned simultaneously.

- **Channels Introduction**: Alongside goroutines, channels were introduced as the primary mechanism for safe communication between these concurrently running routines. Channels ensure that data exchange is synchronized, preventing common concurrency issues such as race conditions.

- **Select Statement**: The evolution continued with the introduction of the `select` statement, enhancing Go's concurrency model by enabling a goroutine to wait on multiple communication operations, further simplifying complex concurrent patterns.

Significant improvements and optimizations to Go's runtime scheduler have been made over the years, allowing it to more efficiently distribute goroutines over available CPU cores, thereby optimizing parallel execution and reducing contention. The scheduler's evolution from a cooperative model, where goroutines had to explicitly cede control to the scheduler, to a preemptive model in later versions, has dramatically improved performance and the responsiveness of Go applications.

The language's standard library has also evolved, introducing packages such as `sync`, `context`, and `io`, which provide higher-level abstractions for dealing with synchronization, cancellation, and blocking I/O operations, respectively. These additions have further simplified the development of concurrent applications in Go.

$$\text{Concurrency Efficiency} = \frac{\text{\# Goroutines}}{\text{Memory Overhead} + \text{CPU Utilization}}$$
(1.1)

The equation above captures the essence of what Go strives to achieve in its concurrency model: maximizing the number of goroutines that can be effectively managed and executed with minimal resources. This has made Go particularly attractive for building high-performance, scalable web servers and microservices where efficient concurrency handling is paramount.

The evolution of concurrency in Go has been marked by a consistent effort to balance performance with simplicity. By drawing from the principles of CSP and adapting these ideas within the context of modern programming requirements, Go has established itself as a powerful tool for developers to harness the full potential of multicore computing.

1.4 Why is Concurrency Important?

Concurrency is not just a luxury in modern software development; it is a necessity. As applications grow in complexity and the amount of data they need to process increases exponentially, the traditional sequential way of executing tasks becomes a bottleneck, hampering performance and scalability. Concurrency offers a solution to this problem by allowing multiple tasks to be executed simultaneously, thus improving the efficiency and responsiveness of applications.

One of the core benefits of concurrency is its ability to enhance the utilization of system resources. Modern computers are equipped with multi-core processors, yet, without concurrency, most applications would only leverage a fraction of the available computing power. By dividing tasks into smaller, independent units of execution, known as concurrent tasks, and distributing them across multiple cores, applications can perform more work in the same amount of time. This not only maximizes the use of hardware but also results in faster execution times for tasks that are inherently parallelizable.

Moreover, concurrency is vital for developing responsive user interfaces. In a single-threaded application, long-running tasks, such as network requests or complex computations, can block the main thread, leading to unresponsive or frozen interfaces. This can frustrate users and negatively impact their experience. Concurrency addresses this issue by offloading such tasks to background threads, allowing the main thread to remain responsive to user interactions. This model of separating the task execution from the user interface logic is fundamental in creating smooth and user-friendly applications.

Concurrency also plays a crucial role in the scalability of web services and applications. As the number of concurrent users grows, the demands on the service increase. Applications that rely on a sequential processing model struggle to scale, as each request is processed one after another, leading to increased response times and potential bottlenecks. By adopting a concurrent processing model, web services can handle multiple requests in parallel, improving throughput and reducing latency. This ability to scale effectively is particularly important in the era of cloud computing, where resources can be dynamically allocated based on demand.

However, embracing concurrency is not without its challenges. The complexity of designing, implementing, and maintaining concurrent programs is significantly higher than that of sequential ones. Issues such as race conditions, deadlocks, and data races introduce bugs that are often difficult to reproduce and debug. Furthermore, the performance gains from concurrency are not always linear and predictable, as overhead from thread management and synchronization can offset the benefits under certain circumstances. Therefore, understanding the principles of concurrent programming and the specific concurrency model of a language, such as Go, is essential for harnessing its full potential.

Concurrency is indispensable in building efficient, responsive, and scalable applications. Go's built-in support for concurrency, through goroutines and channels, provides a powerful set of tools for developers to address the challenges of modern software development. By leveraging these concurrency primitives, developers can write simpler, more maintainable concurrent code that fully utilizes system resources and meets the demands of today's users and systems.

1.5 Go's Approach to Concurrency

Concurrency has always been a cornerstone of software efficiency and performance, particularly in an era dominated by the need for high-speed and real-time processing. Go's approach to concurrency is both innovative and pragmatic, distinguishing it from other programming languages through its simplicity and effectiveness.

At the heart of Go's concurrency model are two key components: goroutines and channels. These elements work in tandem to enable the straightforward creation and management of concurrent operations within Go applications.

Goroutines

Goroutines are lightweight threads managed by the Go runtime. The creation of a goroutine is remarkably simple, achieved by prefixing a function call with the go keyword. Unlike traditional threads, goroutines require significantly less memory overhead and are managed by the Go runtime scheduler, which multiplexes them onto a small number of OS threads.

```
func printNumbers() {
    for i := 1; i <= 5; i++ {
        fmt.Println(i)
    }
}
```

```
6
7   func main() {
8       go printNumbers()
9   }
```

The code snippet above demonstrates the creation of a goroutine to execute the printNumbers function concurrently with the main function. This simplicity in spawning concurrent operations is a defining feature of Go's concurrency model.

Channels

Channels are the conduits through which goroutines communicate and synchronize their execution. They are typed, meaning a channel can transport data of a specific type, enforcing type safety within concurrent operations. Creating a channel in Go is straightforward, using the built-in make function.

```
1   ch := make(chan int)
```

Channels support both sending and receiving operations, which are blocking by nature. This blocking mechanism ensures that data races are avoided, as a goroutine will wait on a send operation until another goroutine is ready to receive the data, and vice versa.

```
1   func sendData(ch chan int) {
2       ch <- 1 // Send data into channel
3   }
4
5   func receiveData(ch chan int) {
6       data := <- ch // Receive data from channel
7       fmt.Println(data)
8   }
9
10  func main() {
11      ch := make(chan int)
12      go sendData(ch)
13      go receiveData(ch)
14  }
```

In the example above, one goroutine sends an integer to the channel, while another goroutine receives that integer from the channel. This interaction underscores the synchronization capability of channels, enabling safe and efficient communication between concurrently executing goroutines.

Select Statement

Go further bolsters its concurrency model with the `select` statement, allowing a program to wait on multiple channel operations. The `select` statement blocks until one of its cases can proceed, making it invaluable for implementing complex synchronization patterns.

```
select {
case msg1 := <-ch1:
    fmt.Println("Received", msg1)
case msg2 := <-ch2:
    fmt.Println("Received", msg2)
case <-time.After(1 * time.Second):
    fmt.Println("Timeout")
}
```

This mechanism is particularly useful for handling timeouts or operating over multiple channels simultaneously, showcasing the depth and flexibility of Go's approach to concurrency.

Advantages of Go's Concurrency Model

Go's concurrency model offers several advantages:

- Simplified concurrent programming model compared to traditional thread-based approaches.

- Efficient execution of thousands of goroutines due to low memory overhead.

- Robust synchronization and communication facilities through channels.

- Enhanced readability and maintainability of concurrent code.

Go's approach to concurrency, characterized by goroutines, channels, and the `select` statement, represents a significant simplification and enhancement over traditional concurrency models. By integrating these features deeply into the language, Go allows developers to build high-performance, scalable, and concurrent applications with relative ease.

1.6   Goroutines: The Building Blocks of Concurrency

Goroutines are at the heart of Go's concurrency model. They are lightweight threads managed by the Go runtime rather than the operating system. This distinction allows for the creation of thousands, even millions, of goroutines on a single machine without the overhead typically associated with traditional threading models. Here, we will delve into the mechanics of goroutines, illustrating how they are created and how they operate within the Go runtime environment.

Creating a goroutine is astonishingly straightforward. It is achieved by simply prefixing a function call with the go keyword. This simplicity belies the complexity of the actions performed by the Go runtime to manage these goroutines efficiently.

```
package main

import (
    "fmt"
    "time"
)

func say(s string) {
    for i := 0; i < 5; i++ {
        time.Sleep(100 * time.Millisecond)
        fmt.Println(s)
    }
}

func main() {
    go say("world")
    say("hello")
}
```

In the above example, main function calls say("hello") directly and say("world") in a new goroutine. The output of this program demonstrates the concurrent execution of both calls to say. It is important to note that when the main function returns, all goroutines are abruptly stopped, regardless of their state.

One of the key advantages of goroutines is their cost-effectiveness in terms of system resources. This efficiency originates from the Go scheduler, an integral part of the Go runtime that multiplexes goroutines onto a smaller number of OS threads. The number of threads used does not need to be equal to the number of goroutines. In fact, many goroutines can run on a single thread thanks to Go's non-blocking I/O operations and the scheduler's intelligent management of goroutine execution.

```
hello
world
hello
world
hello
world
hello
world
hello
```

The output order may vary, highlighting the non-deterministic execution order of goroutines. This is a key characteristic of concurrent programs and underscores the need for synchronization mechanisms when sharing data across goroutines, a topic that we will cover in subsequent sections.

Goroutines communicate with each other using channels. Channels provide a way for goroutines to send and receive messages synchronously or asynchronously, making the management of state across goroutines both safer and easier. The Go runtime's deadlock detection and panic recovery mechanisms are part of what makes goroutines particularly robust for building concurrent applications.

As the foundational building block of concurrency in Go, goroutines represent a powerful abstraction. They enable developers to harness the power of concurrency without getting ensnared in the complexities typically associated with thread management. In subsequent sections, we will explore more advanced aspects of concurrency in Go, including the use of channels to facilitate communication and synchronize the execution between goroutines.

1.7 Simple Goroutine Example

Go's treatment of concurrency is both robust and straightforward, central to which is the concept of goroutines. A goroutine is a lightweight thread managed by the Go runtime, offering a simple yet powerful way to execute functions concurrently. This section will present a basic example of using goroutines, elucidating their ease of implementation and utility.

To commence, consider a function that performs a task, such as printing a message to the console. In a sequential execution context, this function would block any subsequent operations until it completes its execution. However, by invoking this function as a goroutine, execution continues to the next line of code without waiting, thereby allowing multiple operations to occur concurrently.

Here is a simple demonstration:

```
package main

import (
    "fmt"
    "time"
)

// Define a function that will be executed as a goroutine
func printMessage(message string) {
    for i := 0; i < 5; i++ {
        fmt.Println(message)
        // Pause to simulate a time-consuming task
        time.Sleep(time.Millisecond * 100)
    }
}

func main() {
    // Execute printMessage as a goroutine
    go printMessage("Hello from goroutine")

    // Main function continues executing without waiting
    printMessage("Hello from main function")

    // Wait for a key press to end the program
    fmt.Scanln()
    fmt.Println("Program has ended")
}
```

In the above code, the printMessage function is executed twice: once as a goroutine and once in the usual sequential manner. When executed as a goroutine using the go keyword, control immediately returns to the next line in the main function without waiting for printMessage to complete. This simultaneous execution demonstrates the essence of concurrency.

It is worth noting the output of the program may vary from execution to execution due to the concurrent nature of goroutines. The scheduler of the Go runtime manages the execution of goroutines, and it might interleave their execution in a non-deterministic order. As a result, the messages printed to the console may appear in different sequences. An example output might look like this:

```
Hello from main function
Hello from goroutine
Hello from main function
Hello from goroutine
Hello from main function
Hello from goroutine
Hello from main function
Hello from goroutine
Hello from main function
Hello from goroutine
Program has ended
```

This example illustrates the concurrency in Go achieved through goroutines, enabling the program to perform multiple operations seemingly in parallel. It's important to understand that while goroutines facilitate concurrent execution, they do not guarantee parallelism, a distinction that will be discussed in the following sections.

1.8 Understanding Go Scheduler

Concurrency in Go is deeply intertwined with the concept of goroutines, which are lightweight threads managed by the Go runtime rather than the operating system. The efficient scheduling of these goroutines is crucial for achieving the desired concurrency. This is where the Go scheduler plays a pivotal role. Unlike traditional thread schedulers, the Go scheduler is designed with a unique approach to efficiently manage thousands of goroutines concurrently. In this section, we explore the internals of the Go scheduler, its work-stealing algorithm, and how it achieves low-latency scheduling of goroutines.

The Go scheduler implements a M:N scheduling mechanism, where M goroutines are multiplexed onto N OS threads. The primary goal of this mechanism is to keep these OS threads busy with runnable goroutines, while minimizing the overhead associated with thread creation, destruction, and context switching.

- The Go runtime creates several worker OS threads that run on available CPU cores.

- Goroutines are distributed across these worker threads.

- The scheduler dynamically adjusts the allocation of goroutines to threads to achieve optimal performance.

One of the most innovative aspects of the Go scheduler is its work-stealing algorithm. Work stealing is a strategy for balancing the load across multiple worker threads. When a worker thread runs out of jobs, it randomly selects another thread and 'steals' half of its job queue. This ensures that all worker threads have an equal chance of executing goroutines, leading to efficient CPU utilization and reduced latency for concurrent tasks.

The Go scheduler operates in the following manner:

1. When a goroutine makes a blocking system call, the scheduler puts it to sleep and removes it from the thread, allowing another goroutine to take its place and continue execution.

2. In cases where a goroutine is blocked waiting for data from a channel or a network operation, the Go scheduler parks the goroutine and assigns another goroutine to the thread. This 'park and start another' approach prevents the thread from being idle.

3. The scheduler frequently checks for goroutines that have finished waiting and quickly schedules them for execution on available threads.

This approach ensures that the runtime maximizes CPU utilization while minimizing the time goroutines spend waiting for resources or execution.

```
1  // Example of launching a goroutine
2  go func() {
3      fmt.Println("Executing a concurrent task")
4  }()
```

Executing a concurrent task

The scheduler's efficiency largely comes from maintaining a separate run queue of goroutines for each thread and a global run queue. Goroutines are initially placed in the global run queue and then distributed to thread-specific run queues. The work-stealing algorithm functions by allowing idle threads to steal goroutines from the global queue or from other threads' run queues.

$$\text{Efficiency} = \frac{\text{Total Time Active}}{\text{Total Time Available}} \tag{1.2}$$

The equation above highlights a simplified metric for assessing the scheduler's efficiency—balancing the time goroutines are actively running against the overall time they could potentially be running. The closer this ratio is to 1, the higher the efficiency of the scheduler.

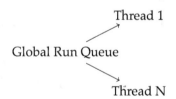

The diagram above represents the distribution process of goroutines from the global run queue to individual thread run queues. This illustrates the multiplexing (M:N scheduling) of goroutines onto OS threads facilitated by the Go scheduler.

The Go scheduler plays a fundamental role in realizing Go's concurrency model.   Its   design   considerations—like   the

27

work-stealing   algorithm   and   the   M:N   scheduling mechanism—allow developers to write highly concurrent programs without delving into the intricate details of thread management. Understanding the Go scheduler's working mechanism provides insights into the performance characteristics of Go programs and helps in writing efficient and scalable concurrent applications.

1.9   Challenges of Concurrent Programming

Concurrency, while powerful, introduces a unique set of challenges that can complicate software development. Understanding these difficulties is crucial for developers aiming to create efficient and error-free concurrent programs in Go. This section will discuss the primary challenges encountered in concurrent programming, including race conditions, deadlock, starvation, and managing shared state.

Race Conditions

A race condition occurs when two or more operations must execute in the correct order for the program to function as intended, but the program does not enforce this order, leading to unpredictable results.

Consider the example where two goroutines update the same global counter:

```
1   var counter int
2
3   func increment() {
4       counter++
5   }
6
7   func main() {
8       go increment()
9       go increment()
10  }
```

In the absence of synchronization mechanisms, there is no guarantee which 'increment' operation will execute first. As a result, the final value of counter might not reflect the expected outcome after two increments.

Deadlock

Deadlock is a situation where two or more goroutines are waiting on each other to release resources, but none of them actually do, causing the program to hang indefinitely. This typically occurs in complex resource sharing situations or when improper lock handling is implemented.

An illustrative deadlock scenario is as follows:

```
func deadlockExample() {
    lockA := &sync.Mutex{}
    lockB := &sync.Mutex{}

    go func() {
        lockA.Lock()
        defer lockA.Unlock()

        time.Sleep(1 * time.Second) // Simulate work

        lockB.Lock()
        defer lockB.Unlock()

        // More work
    }()

    go func() {
        lockB.Lock()
        defer lockB.Unlock()

        time.Sleep(1 * time.Second) // Simulate work

        lockA.Lock()
        defer lockA.Unlock()

        // More work
    }()
}
```

In this example, each goroutine acquires one lock and then waits to acquire the other, leading to a situation where neither can progress.

Starvation

Starvation occurs when one or more goroutines are prevented from making progress because other goroutines are monopolizing resources. This often results from priority inversion or poor lock management, where lower priority tasks hold resources needed by higher priority tasks indefinitely or for prolonged periods.

Managing Shared State

Effective management of shared state is pivotal in concurrent programming. Improper handling can easily lead to issues such as race conditions. Using mutexes (sync.Mutex) and channels are common strategies to manage shared state safely.

For instance, to safely update a shared counter, one could use a mutex as follows:

```
1  var mutex sync.Mutex
2  var counter int
3
4  func safeIncrement() {
5      mutex.Lock()
6      defer mutex.Unlock()
7      counter++
8  }
```

This ensures that at any given time, only one goroutine can update counter, thus preventing race conditions.

In summary, while concurrency offers numerous benefits in terms of performance and responsiveness, it also requires careful consideration and handling of potential pitfalls such as race conditions, deadlock, starvation, and managing shared state. Understanding and addressing these challenges is essential for successful concurrent programming in Go.

1.10 Preview of Concurrent Patterns in Go

In this section, we will discuss some of the commonly utilized concurrent patterns in Go programming. These patterns offer structured approaches to solving common concurrency challenges, facilitating the development of efficient, scalable, and maintainable code. By understanding and applying these patterns, developers can more easily harness the power of Go's concurrency features.

Worker Pools

The worker pool pattern, also known as the goroutine pool pattern, involves the creation of a fixed number of goroutines to perform tasks concurrently. This pattern is particularly useful for managing resources efficiently and limiting the overhead associated with creating and destroying a large number of goroutines. It is implemented by creating a channel to which tasks are sent and a pool of worker goroutines that process these tasks.

```
1   type Job func()
2
3   func startWorkerPool(workerCount int, jobs <-chan Job) {
4       for i := 0; i < workerCount; i++ {
5           go func() {
6               for job := range jobs {
7                   job()
8               }
9           }()
10      }
11  }
```

In the example above, `startWorkerPool` creates a specified number of worker goroutines. Each worker listens to the jobs channel, executing any received Job functions.

Pipeline

A pipeline is a pattern where the output of one process serves as the input to another, forming a chain of processing elements. In Go, this is elegantly implemented using channels, where multiple stages of processing are connected through channels, and each stage is handled by goroutines. Pipelines are beneficial for processing streams of data with clearly defined stages.

```go
func generator(numbers ...int) <-chan int {
    out := make(chan int)
    go func() {
        for _, n := range numbers {
            out <- n
        }
        close(out)
    }()
    return out
}

func square(in <-chan int) <-chan int {
    out := make(chan int)
    go func() {
        for n := range in {
            out <- n * n
        }
        close(out)
    }()
    return out
}
```

In this pipeline example, `generator` emits numbers into a channel, which are then squared by the `square` function. The use of channels facilitates the flow of data between different stages of the pipeline.

Fan-In and Fan-Out

The fan-out pattern involves starting multiple goroutines to handle input from a single channel, effectively distributing work amongst a set of workers to parallelize CPU- and I/O-bound tasks. Conversely, the fan-in pattern involves combining multiple input channels into a single channel. These patterns are crucial for increasing throughput and efficiency.

```go
func fanOutIn(in <-chan int) <-chan int {
    var workers int = 10
    channels := make([]<-chan int, workers)
    for i := 0; i < workers; i++ {
        channels[i] = square(in)
    }
    return fanIn(channels...)
}
```

```
10   func fanIn(channels ...<-chan int) <-chan int {
11      var wg sync.WaitGroup
12      merged := make(chan int)
13      output := func(c <-chan int) {
14         for n := range c {
15            merged <- n
16         }
17         wg.Done()
18      }
19      wg.Add(len(channels))
20      for _, c := range channels {
21         go output(c)
22      }
23      go func() {
24         wg.Wait()
25         close(merged)
26      }()
27      return merged
28   }
```

In the fan-out, fan-in example above, `square` functions are executed in parallel across multiple channels, after which their outputs are combined.

By embracing these concurrent patterns, developers can effectively tackle common concurrency problems and enhance the performance of Go applications. Each pattern offers a different approach to structuring concurrent code, allowing for flexibility in addressing various software design challenges.

Chapter 2

Understanding Goroutines

Goroutines are at the heart of Go's concurrency model, providing a lightweight and efficient way to handle concurrent tasks within a program. Unlike traditional threads, goroutines are managed by the Go runtime, offering significant savings in terms of memory and setup time, which in turn facilitates the development of highly concurrent applications. This chapter delves into creating, understanding, and effectively utilizing goroutines, covering their operation, comparison with threads, and synchronization techniques necessary for safe concurrent execution. With a focus on practical examples and best practices, readers will gain the knowledge needed to implement goroutines in their Go applications confidently.

2.1   Introduction to Goroutines

Goroutines are a fundamental concept in Go's approach to concurrency. They are functions or methods that run concurrently with other goroutines within a single Go process.   Unlike heavyweight operating system threads, goroutines are multiplexed onto a small number of OS threads by the Go runtime scheduler. This design allows for the creation of thousands of goroutines without incurring the substantial overhead associated with traditional thread models.

Creating a goroutine is straightforward. It is done by prepending the keyword go before a function call. This simplicity belies the underlying complexity managed by the Go runtime, making concurrent programming more accessible and less error-prone for developers. Consider the following illustrative example:

```
1   package main
2
3   import (
4       "fmt"
5       "time"
6   )
7
8   func say(s string) {
9       for i := 0; i < 5; i++ {
10          time.Sleep(100 * time.Millisecond)
11          fmt.Println(s)
12      }
13  }
14
15  func main() {
16      go say("world")
17      say("hello")
18  }
```

In the example above, two say functions are executed concurrently. When the program is run, the output interleaves the prints of "hello" and "world", demonstrating concurrent execution.

A critical aspect of goroutines is their cost-effectiveness. Traditional threads require a significant amount of memory per instance, typically on the order of megabytes. In contrast, a goroutine initially only needs a few kilobytes of stack space. The stack grows and shrinks as needed, further optimizing memory usage. This efficiency is a key enabler of Go's lightweight concurrency model.

The lifecycle of a goroutine is managed entirely by the Go runtime, abstracting away the complexities associated with creating, scheduling, and terminating traditional threads. This abstraction allows developers to focus on the logic of their concurrent tasks rather than the intricacies of thread management.

It is also worth noting the non-preemptive nature of Go's scheduler. Goroutines yield control to the scheduler at specific points in their execution, such as during I/O operations, channel operations, or when explicitly calling runtime functions designed to yield. This cooperative scheduling model contributes to the efficiency of goroutine execution but also requires careful consideration when designing concurrent programs to avoid deadlocks or excessive blocking.

In summary, goroutines represent a powerful yet user-friendly approach to concurrency. Their design allows developers to create highly concurrent applications with minimal overhead, both in terms of performance and cognitive load. Understanding the operation and best practices of goroutines is essential for leveraging the full capabilities of Go as a modern, concurrent programming language.

2.2 Creating Your First Goroutine

Creating your first goroutine is a straightforward task yet an essential step towards harnessing the power of concurrency in Go. A goroutine is a lightweight thread of execution managed by the Go runtime, allowing developers to execute functions concurrently. This section will guide you through the process of creating and executing your first goroutine, along with an explanation of the underlying principles that make goroutines an efficient tool for writing concurrent programs.

To initiate a goroutine, you use the go keyword followed by the function call you wish to execute concurrently. It is important to note that the function will now run in parallel with the other code without blocking its execution. Here is a basic example:

```
1   package main
2
3   import (
4       "fmt"
5       "time"
6   )
7
```

```
8   func printNumbers() {
9       for i := 1; i <= 5; i++ {
10          time.Sleep(100 * time.Millisecond)
11          fmt.Println(i)
12      }
13  }
14
15  func main() {
16      go printNumbers()
17      fmt.Println("Started printing numbers in a goroutine.")
18      time.Sleep(1 * time.Second) // give enough time for goroutine to finish
19      fmt.Println("Finished executing the main function.")
20  }
```

In the code above, printNumbers is a function that simply prints numbers 1 through 5, pausing for 100 milliseconds after printing each number. In the main function, the go keyword precedes the printNumbers function call, indicating that it should run as a goroutine. This means the main function will continue executing without waiting for printNumbers to complete, hence the need for the time.Sleep call at the end of main to prevent the program from exiting before printNumbers has finished executing.

It's crucial to understand that despite their simplicity, goroutines are not executed in a guaranteed sequence. The Go runtime schedules their execution, which can lead to nondeterministic behavior in the order of operations. Therefore, synchronization mechanisms, which will be discussed in later sections, are key to controlling access to shared resources and ensuring that goroutines interact in a predictable manner.

Understanding Goroutine Startup

When a goroutine is started using the go keyword, the Go runtime creates a stack for the goroutine to use. This stack is not fixed in size and can grow or shrink based on the needs of the goroutine, making goroutines extremely memory efficient compared to traditional threads.

After creation, the goroutine is scheduled to run on one of the available logical CPUs. The actual timing of its execution depends on the Go scheduler, which is a part of the Go runtime tasked with distributing goroutines over the available CPUs for execution.

Running multiple goroutines concurrently does not necessarily mean they will execute at the same time. Concurrency is about dealing with multiple tasks at once. Whether tasks are carried out simultaneously depends on the number of CPUs available and how the Go scheduler manages goroutine execution.

```
Started printing numbers in a goroutine.
1
2
3
4
5
Finished executing the main function.
```

The output above illustrates that the goroutine printNumbers runs concurrently with the main function. However, due to the sleep in main, the printNumbers function has enough time to complete its execution before the program terminates.

This section has provided a foundational understanding of creating and executing your first goroutine. By following the provided example, you can start experimenting with goroutines and explore the concurrency features offered by Go.

2.3   How Goroutines Work Under the Hood

Goroutines operate differently from traditional threads found in other programming languages. To fully leverage the power of goroutines, a comprehensive understanding of their internal mechanics is crucial. This section will break down the key components and processes that enable the lightweight concurrency model of goroutines.

Firstly, it's essential to clarify the concept of a goroutine in the context of the Go programming language. A goroutine is a function executing concurrently with other goroutines in the same address space. It's managed by the Go runtime rather than the operating system, setting it apart from traditional threads which are managed by the kernel.

Goroutine Stack

Each goroutine is allocated a small stack at creation, which grows and shrinks as needed. The initial size of a goroutine stack is typically 2KB, significantly smaller than the default stack size for a traditional thread, usually around 1MB. This small initial size is one reason why the creation of goroutines is less resource-intensive, allowing a single process to manage thousands of goroutines concurrently.

```
1  func myGoroutine() {
2      // Goroutine stack starts small and grows as needed
3  }
```

When a goroutine's stack reaches its maximum capacity, the Go runtime automatically allocates a larger stack and copies the existing stack's data to the new one. This automatic resizing mechanism ensures that even complex, recursive functions can execute within a goroutine without causing a stack overflow.

Goroutine Scheduler

The Go runtime includes a scheduler, implemented in software, that manages the execution of goroutines. The scheduler's main job is to distribute runnable goroutines over multiple operating system threads, so they can execute concurrently on available CPU cores. The scheduler uses a technique known as *work stealing* to balance the load across threads.

```
1  go myGoroutine() // Schedules the myGoroutine for concurrent execution
```

The scheduler employs a *M:N scheduling* model, where M goroutines are multiplexed onto N OS threads. This model allows the scheduler to efficiently manage thousands of goroutines, even if the number of threads is far smaller than the number of goroutines.

Goroutines and Channels

Communication between goroutines is facilitated through channels, a type-safe mechanism that allows goroutines to synchronize with each other without explicit locks or condition variables.

```
1  ch := make(chan int) // Create a new channel of type int
2
3  go func() {
4      ch <- 42 // Send a value into the channel
5  }()
6
7  value := <-ch // Receive a value from the channel
```

Channels can be used to ensure that data dependencies between goroutines are properly managed, preventing common concurrency issues such as race conditions.

Goroutines and Select Statement

The select statement provides another powerful tool for managing goroutines. It allows a goroutine to wait on multiple communication operations, proceeding with the first one that becomes available.

```
1  select {
2  case msg1 := <-ch1:
3      fmt.Println("Received", msg1)
4  case msg2 := <-ch2:
5      fmt.Println("Received", msg2)
6  }
```

By understanding the internal workings of goroutines, developers can write more efficient and robust concurrent Go programs. This knowledge aids in optimally structuring programs to leverage the lightweight concurrency that goroutines offer.

2.4 Goroutines vs. Threads

When it comes to concurrent programming, the terms 'goroutine' and 'thread' often emerge, prompting a comparative analysis of these two fundamental concepts. Understanding the distinctions and similarities between goroutines and threads is crucial for any developer navigating through the realm of concurrent applications in Go.

Threads, on one hand, are a well-established mechanism for achieving concurrency in programming. A thread is the smallest sequence of programmed instructions that can be managed independently by a scheduler, which is typically part of the operating system. Each thread has its own stack, a set of CPU registers, and a program counter. Threads within the same process share the same heap space. This shared memory model allows threads to communicate and share data more easily, but it also introduces complexity in ensuring data consistency and handling race conditions.

Goroutines, on the other hand, are Go's approach to concurrency. They are functions or methods that run concurrently with other functions or methods. Goroutines are managed by the Go runtime rather than the operating system. A key feature of goroutines is their efficiency: they have a much smaller memory footprint compared to threads, often taking up only a few kilobytes. This efficiency allows a Go program to spawn thousands or even millions of goroutines on a single machine.

The contrast between goroutines and threads can be further elaborated in terms of their creation, management, scheduling, and communication mechanisms.

- **Creation and Management:** Threads are directly managed by the operating system, which typically involves significant overhead for creation, destruction, and switching between threads. In contrast, goroutines are managed by the Go runtime, which employs a lightweight mechanism for creating and destroying goroutines. This difference significantly reduces the cost of concurrent operations in Go.

- **Scheduling:** The operating system kernel performs scheduling for threads, often using complex algorithms that take into account thread priorities and CPU time slicing. Goroutines, however, are multiplexed onto a smaller number of OS threads by the Go runtime scheduler. The Go scheduler employs a simpler, cooperative scheduling model, where goroutines yield control back to the scheduler at well-defined points, such as when blocking on IO operations or when explicitly calling the `runtime.Gosched` function.

- **Communication:** Threads often rely on shared memory models for communication, necessitating the use of synchronization primitives like mutexes or semaphores to avoid data races. Goroutines, conversely, typically use channels to communicate, which provides a powerful and flexible mechanism for passing data between concurrently running functions. Channels in Go encourage a pattern of "do not communicate by sharing memory; instead, share memory by communicating," which can lead to more robust and easier-to-understand concurrent code.

- **Stack Size:** Threads typically have a fixed stack size that is allocated when the thread is created, which can be a limiting factor for applications that require deep recursion or a large number of threads. Goroutines start with a small stack that grows and shrinks as needed, making more efficient use of memory and allowing for the creation of a larger number of concurrent entities.

It's essential to understand these differences to harness the full potential of concurrency in Go effectively. By embracing goroutines and the patterns of communication they enable, developers can build highly scalable and maintainable concurrent applications.

2.5 Communicating between Goroutines

Communicating between goroutines is a fundamental aspect of building concurrent applications in Go. Go provides a robust and elegant way to handle this communication through channels. Channels are a typed conduit through which you can send and receive values with the channel operator, <-. This allows goroutines to synchronize execution and safely share data among each other, avoiding common pitfalls of concurrency such as race conditions.

The primary mechanism for managing goroutine communication is the make function, which can create channels of a specific type. These channels are used to transfer data between goroutines. It is important to understand the two types of channels: unbuffered and buffered.

Unbuffered Channels

Unbuffered channels do not store any values. A send operation on an unbuffered channel will block until another goroutine is ready to receive the value, ensuring that two goroutines synchronize. Similarly, a receive operation will block until a value is sent to the channel. This direct hand-off ensures that the operation is always immediate and synchronous.

Consider the following example where two goroutines communicate via an unbuffered channel:

```
1   package main
2
3   import (
4       "fmt"
5       "time"
6   )
7
8   func sendMessage(ch chan string) {
9       ch <- "Hello, World!"
10  }
11
12  func main() {
13      messageChannel := make(chan string)
14      go sendMessage(messageChannel)
15      message := <-messageChannel
16      fmt.Println(message)
17      time.Sleep(time.Second * 1)
18  }
```

44

Buffered Channels

Buffered channels, on the other hand, have a capacity, allowing them to store multiple values before blocking. When the channel's buffer is full, a send operation will block until a value is removed. Similarly, if the channel is empty, a receive operation will block. Buffered channels provide more flexibility but can introduce complexity, as you must manage the buffer size carefully to avoid deadlocks.

Below is an example demonstrating the use of a buffered channel:

```
package main

import "fmt"

func main() {
    messageChannel := make(chan string, 2)
    messageChannel <- "Hello"
    messageChannel <- "World"

    fmt.Println(<-messageChannel)
    fmt.Println(<-messageChannel)
}
```

Select Statement

The select statement in Go is a powerful feature, enabling a goroutine to wait on multiple communication operations. The select blocks until one of its cases can proceed, making it an efficient way to handle multiple channels simultaneously. It is notably useful when dealing with timeouts or cancellation signals.

Here is a simple example using the select statement:

```
package main

import (
    "fmt"
    "time"
)

func main() {
    ch1 := make(chan string)
```

```
10     ch2 := make(chan string)
11
12     go func() {
13         time.Sleep(2 * time.Second)
14         ch1 <- "Message from ch1"
15     }()
16
17     go func() {
18         time.Sleep(1 * time.Second)
19         ch2 <- "Message from ch2"
20     }()
21
22     for i := 0; i < 2; i++ {
23         select {
24         case msg1 := <-ch1:
25             fmt.Println(msg1)
26         case msg2 := <-ch2:
27             fmt.Println(msg2)
28         }
29     }
30 }
```

This example demonstrates concurrent operations, waiting for messages from two different channels. The select statement efficiently handles whichever channel is ready to communicate first.

Closing Channels

Channels need to be closed only when there is a necessity to indicate that no more values will be sent on the channel. Closing a channel is done using the close function. Receivers can test whether a channel has been closed by assigning a second parameter to the receive expression, which is a boolean value indicating whether the receive operation was successful.

```
1 package main
2
3 import (
4     "fmt"
5 )
6
7 func main() {
8     ch := make(chan int, 5)
```

```
 9    for i := 0; i < 5; i++ {
10        ch <- i
11    }
12    close(ch)
13
14    for i := range ch {
15        fmt.Println(i)
16    }
17  }
```

This code snippet populates a channel with five integers, then closes the channel. The range loop iterates over each element until the channel is closed, displaying each integer.

Channels are a powerful tool for communication between goroutines, providing a means to safely share data and synchronize execution in concurrent Go applications. By understanding how to use unbuffered and buffered channels, the select statement, and when to close channels appropriately, developers can build sophisticated and efficient concurrent systems.

2.6 Synchronization Techniques

Goroutines provide a powerful model for concurrent execution in Go programs. However, when multiple goroutines access shared resources, there is a potential for data races and other synchronization issues. To ensure the correctness and safety of concurrent applications, Go offers several synchronization primitives. This section explores the use of channels, sync package, and atomic operations to synchronize goroutines effectively.

Channels for Synchronization

Channels in Go are not only a means for communication between goroutines but can also be used for synchronization. A key feature of channels is the ability to block a goroutine's execution until an operation on the channel can proceed. This behavior is instrumental in coordinating goroutines.

```
1   package main
2
3   import (
4       "fmt"
5       "time"
6   )
7
8   func worker(done chan bool) {
9       fmt.Print("Working...")
10      time.Sleep(time.Second)
11      fmt.Println("done")
12
13      // Notify that we're done.
14      done <- true
15  }
16
17  func main() {
18      done := make(chan bool, 1)
19      go worker(done)
20
21      // Block until we receive a notification from the worker
22      <-done
23  }
```

```
Working...done
```

In the example above, the main function launches a goroutine and waits for it to finish by blocking on the done channel. The worker goroutine sends a value on this channel once it has completed its work, thus unblocking the main function.

The sync Package

The sync package provides additional synchronization primitives such as Mutex, RWMutex, WaitGroup, and others. These primitives are useful for more complex synchronization scenarios that cannot be easily handled with channels alone.

Using Mutex for Mutual Exclusion

Mutex provides a mutual exclusion lock, allowing goroutines to safely access shared resources by ensuring only one goroutine can access the resource at a time.

```
1   package main
2
3   import (
4       "fmt"
5       "sync"
6   )
7
8   var count int
9   var mutex sync.Mutex
10
11  func increment() {
12      mutex.Lock()
13      count++
14      mutex.Unlock()
15  }
16
17  func main() {
18      var wg sync.WaitGroup
19      for i := 0; i < 1000; i++ {
20          wg.Add(1)
21          go func() {
22              increment()
23              wg.Done()
24          }()
25      }
26      wg.Wait()
27      fmt.Println("Count:", count)
28  }
```

Count: 1000

WaitGroups for Goroutine Completion

WaitGroup is used to wait for a collection of goroutines to finish executing. It is particularly useful when the number of goroutines to wait on is not known at compile time.

```
1   package main
2
3   import (
4       "fmt"
5       "sync"
6   )
7
8   func worker(id int, wg *sync.WaitGroup) {
9       defer wg.Done()
10      fmt.Printf("Worker %d starting\n", id)
11      // Perform work...
12      fmt.Printf("Worker %d done\n", id)
13  }
```

49

```
14
15   func main() {
16       var wg sync.WaitGroup
17       for i := 1; i <= 5; i++ {
18           wg.Add(1)
19           go worker(i, &wg)
20       }
21       wg.Wait()
22   }
```

```
Worker 1 starting
Worker 2 starting
Worker 3 starting
Worker 4 starting
Worker 5 starting
Worker 1 done
Worker 2 done
Worker 3 done
Worker 4 done
Worker 5 done
```

Atomic Operations

For simple state management, Go's sync/atomic package offers low-level atomic memory primitives. These operations allow for safe manipulation of types such as int32, int64, uint32, uint64, uintptr, and pointers, without the need for Mutex locks.

```
1    package main
2
3    import (
4        "fmt"
5        "sync"
6        "sync/atomic"
7    )
8
9    var counter int64
10
11   func increment(wg *sync.WaitGroup) {
12       atomic.AddInt64(&counter, 1)
13       wg.Done()
14   }
15
16   func main() {
17       var wg sync.WaitGroup
18       for i := 0; i < 1000; i++ {
19           wg.Add(1)
20           go increment(&wg)
21       }
22       wg.Wait()
```

```
23    fmt.Println("Counter:", atomic.LoadInt64(&counter))
24  }
```

```
Counter: 1000
```

In this example, `atomic.AddInt64` safely increments the `counter` variable concurrently from multiple goroutines. Atomic operations are a low-overhead synchronization method for simple state updates.

Go provides a robust set of primitives for synchronizing goroutines. Channels, mutexes, wait groups, and atomic operations each serve different synchronization needs. Understanding when and how to use these primitives is crucial for developing correct and efficient concurrent Go programs.

2.7 Goroutine Lifecycle

Understanding the lifecycle of a goroutine is fundamental in mastering concurrent programming in Go. The lifecycle of a goroutine outlines its creation, execution, and termination phases, offering insights into how these elements can be effectively managed within Go applications.

To start, the creation of a goroutine is initiated by the go keyword followed by a function call. This simplicity is deceptive, as the action sets in motion a series of complex interactions within the Go runtime. Consider the following example:

```
1  go func() {
2      fmt.Println("Executing in a goroutine")
3  }()
```

This snippet creates a goroutine that executes the anonymous function, printing a message to the console. The creation phase is almost instantaneous, demonstrating how lightweight and efficient goroutines are when compared to traditional threads.

Once created, a goroutine enters the execution phase. During this phase, the Go runtime scheduler assigns the goroutine to an available thread in the thread pool. The scheduler in Go is a M:N scheduler, meaning it multiplexes M goroutines onto N OS threads. This model is crucial for understanding its efficiency, as the runtime can dynamically manage goroutines and threads, leveraging the available computing resources optimally.

Goroutines yield control back to the scheduler in three main scenarios, contributing to the non-preemptive nature of goroutine execution:

- When a goroutine performs a blocking I/O operation.

- By explicitly calling the runtime.Gosched() function, which allows other goroutines to run.

- When a goroutine attempts to make a channel operation that cannot proceed immediately.

The termination phase of a goroutine is implicitly initiated once the function it is executing returns. This design means that there are no manual cleanup operations required by the developer, as the Go runtime handles the lifecycle end. It's important to note that if the main goroutine (the one that runs the main() function) terminates, the program exits, and any still-running goroutines are abruptly stopped:

```
func main() {
    go func() {
        fmt.Println("This might not execute.")
    }()
}
```

In this case, there's a chance that the program will exit before the goroutine has a chance to execute. This behavior underlines the importance of synchronization techniques, such as using WaitGroups or channels, to ensure that main waits for all goroutines to complete before exiting.

Moreover, understanding the lifecycle allows for better debugging and performance tuning. For instance, analyzing why a goroutine is stuck in the execution phase might reveal resource contention or deadlocks, leading to more robust and efficient Go applications.

Mastering the goroutine lifecycle is pivotal for effective concurrent programming in Go. By understanding the creation, execution, and termination phases, developers can leverage the full potential of Go's concurrency model, writing applications that are both powerful and efficient.

2.8   Best Practices for Using Goroutines

Employing goroutines in Go applications enhances concurrency, making programs more efficient and responsive. However, to fully leverage their potential without introducing bugs or performance issues, it is crucial to adhere to certain best practices. This section will detail these practices, providing guidance for the effective use of goroutines.

- **Keep the number of goroutines manageable**: While goroutines are lightweight compared to threads, indiscriminate spawning of thousands or millions of goroutines can lead to performance degradation. It is advisable to monitor the number of active goroutines using tools like the Go runtime's `runtime.NumGoroutine()` function and maintain a balance that suits the application's requirements and the system's capabilities.

- **Use synchronization primitives correctly**: Goroutines often access shared data, necessitating proper synchronization to avoid race conditions. The Go standard library provides several synchronization primitives, such as Mutexes (`sync.Mutex`), Channels (`chan`), and Wait Groups (`sync.WaitGroup`). Choose the appropriate primitive based on the use case:

  - Use Mutexes for protecting shared states.

  - Channels are ideal for passing data between goroutines.

  - Wait Groups help in waiting for a collection of goroutines to finish executing.

- **Prefer channels for goroutine communication**: Channels are
  a powerful feature in Go for goroutine-to-goroutine communication. They provide a synchronous or asynchronous way to
  send and receive data, making code easier to understand and
  safer from deadlocks when used correctly. The following code
  snippet demonstrates creating a channel, sending, and receiving data.

```
1  ch := make(chan int) // Create a channel of int
2  go func() {
3      ch <- 42 // Sending data to channel
4  }()
5  value := <-ch // Receiving data from channel
6  println(value)
```

The output of the code snippet would look like this:

42

- **Implement graceful shutdown of goroutines**: An essential
  practice in using goroutines is ensuring they can be stopped
  gracefully, especially in long-running applications or those
  requiring   cleanup   operations   before   termination.
  Implementing a cancellation mechanism, such as using a
  `context.Context` with a cancellation function, provides a
  way to signal goroutines to terminate their execution
  promptly and safely.

- **Avoid goroutine leaks**: Goroutines that are no longer needed
  but still running in the background constitute a leak, potentially
  leading to resource exhaustion. To prevent this, always ensure
  that goroutines terminate, either by reaching the end of their
  function or by receiving a termination signal through a channel
  or context.

- **Profile and monitor goroutine performance**:   Regular
  profiling of goroutine performance using Go's built-in tools,
  such as the `pprof` package, can help identify bottlenecks,
  memory leaks, or excessive CPU usage.   Monitoring these
  metrics provides insights into the application's performance
  and guides optimization efforts.

- **Test concurrent code thoroughly**: Testing is crucial, especially in concurrent applications where bugs can be elusive and hard to reproduce. The Go standard library offers the `testing` package, which supports writing unit tests, including those for concurrent code. Use the `-race` flag during testing to help detect race conditions.

Adhering to these best practices when using goroutines will not only enhance the performance and reliability of Go applications but also streamline the development process, making it easier to write, debug, and maintain concurrent code.

2.9 Common Mistakes with Goroutines

Handling concurrency with goroutines represents a powerful capability within the Go language, enabling developers to craft highly responsive and concurrent applications. Yet, the misuse or misunderstanding of this feature can lead to common pitfalls that may affect performance, lead to deadlocks, or cause unexpected behavior in your programs. This section aims to shed light on these common mistakes when working with goroutines and provides guidance on how to avoid them.

Ignoring Goroutine Leakage

One of the most prevalent issues arises when goroutines are spawned without an eventual termination path. This scenario, known as goroutine leakage, results in an ever-increasing number of idle goroutines that consume system resources unnecessarily.

To mitigate goroutine leakage, ensure each goroutine has a clear and reachable exit path. This can be achieved by utilizing context cancellation, channel signaling, or timeout mechanisms to signal a goroutine to terminate its execution once its job is done or no longer needed.

```
1  ctx, cancel := context.WithCancel(context.Background())
```

```
 2
 3   go func() {
 4       select {
 5       case <-ctx.Done():
 6           // Cleanup and exit the goroutine
 7           return
 8       // Other case branches for regular operation
 9       }
10   }()
11
12   // When the goroutine needs to be stopped:
13   cancel()
```

Misunderstanding Goroutine Scheduling

Goroutines, while lightweight, are not executed in parallel by default. The Go scheduler multiplexes goroutines onto a smaller set of OS threads, meaning that without proper design, goroutines may not run as concurrently as expected, especially on single-core systems.

It is crucial to design your goroutine usage with the Go scheduler in mind. Utilize concurrency primitives such as channels or the sync package to orchestrate goroutine execution and leverage GOMAXPROCS to adjust the number of OS threads used for executing goroutines:

```
1   import "runtime"
2
3   func init() {
4       runtime.GOMAXPROCS(4)
5   }
```

Data Race Conditions

Data races occur when two or more goroutines attempt to access the same variable concurrently, and at least one of the accesses is a write.   Data races can lead to unpredictable behavior and challenging to trace bugs.

To prevent data races, use synchronization primitives provided by the Go language, such as mutexes, channels, or the atomic package, to safely manage access to shared resources:

```
1    var mu sync.Mutex
2    var counter int
3
4    func increment() {
5        mu.Lock()
6        counter++
7        mu.Unlock()
8    }
9
10   go increment()
11   go increment()
```

Overlooking Deadlocks and Livelocks

Deadlocks occur when goroutines are stuck waiting on each other, leading to a complete standstill, whereas livelocks are situations where goroutines continuously change states in response to each other without making progress.

Detecting and resolving deadlocks and livelocks involves careful analysis of the goroutines' interaction patterns, ensuring no circular dependencies exist, and that there are timeouts or cancellations paths for tasks that may get stuck.

Unbuffered Channels for Control Flow

Using unbuffered channels for control flow between goroutines might lead to unexpected behavior or deadlocks, especially if the goroutines' execution depends on the receiving end being ready or vice versa.

To circumvent this, consider using buffered channels with a capacity that matches the expected concurrency level or redesigning the interaction to avoid tight coupling between goroutines.

```
1    done := make(chan bool, 1)
2
3    go func() {
4        // Perform task
5        done <- true
6    }()
7
8    <-done
```

While goroutines are a cornerstone of concurrent programming in Go, they come with their challenges and pitfalls. Recognizing and avoiding these common mistakes will greatly enhance the robustness and efficiency of your Go applications.

2.10   Debugging Goroutines

Debugging concurrent applications in Go, particularly those that make extensive use of goroutines, presents a unique set of challenges. Given the nature of concurrent execution, traditional debugging techniques may not always yield the expected insights. However, Go provides several powerful tools and methodologies to simplify the process. This section explores key strategies for debugging applications that utilize goroutines, highlighting the use of runtime analysis tools, logging, and race condition detectors.

Leveraging the Go Runtime

The Go runtime incorporates built-in facilities that are instrumental for debugging concurrent applications. These include the `runtime` and `pprof` packages, which offer comprehensive insights into the execution state of goroutines.

Runtime Stack Inspection

The `runtime` package can be employed to inspect the stack traces of all goroutines in a program. This is particularly useful for identifying deadlocks or scenarios where goroutines are blocked indefinitely. The following example demonstrates how to print the stack trace of all goroutines:

```
1  package main
2
3  import (
4      "runtime"
5      "fmt"
6  )
7
```

```
8    func main() {
9        go func() {
10           fmt.Println("Executing a goroutine")
11       }()
12
13       // Obtain stack trace
14       buf := make([]byte, 1024)
15       n := runtime.Stack(buf, true)
16       fmt.Println(string(buf[:n]))
17   }
```

In the example above, the runtime.Stack function is called with a byte slice to populate with the stack trace, and a boolean argument indicating that all goroutines' stack traces should be included. The stack trace is then printed, providing a snapshot of the running goroutines' state.

Profiling with pprof

For more in-depth analysis, the pprof package offers profiling capabilities that can be used to identify performance bottlenecks and understand how goroutines are scheduled and executed. To illustrate, the following snippet sets up an HTTP server that exposes runtime profiling data:

```
1    package main
2
3    import (
4        _ "net/http/pprof"
5        "net/http"
6    )
7
8    func main() {
9        go func() {
10           for {
11               // Simulate work
12           }
13       }()
14
15       http.ListenAndServe(":8080", nil)
16   }
```

By navigating to http://localhost:8080/debug/pprof/goroutine, developers can access a profile that enumerates the goroutines in the application.

Detecting Race Conditions

Concurrency bugs, especially race conditions, are notoriously difficult to diagnose and rectify. The Go runtime includes the -race flag
that can be passed to the go run, go build, or go test commands to
enable the race detector. This tool performs a dynamic analysis of the
application, reporting race conditions that are detected at runtime:

```
==================
WARNING: DATA RACE
Read at 0x00c0000b4008 by goroutine 7:
  main.main.func1()
      /path/to/file.go:10 +0x3e

Previous write at 0x00c0000b4008 by main goroutine:
  main.main()
      /path/to/file.go:8 +0x6a
==================
```

The output provides detailed information about the conflicting
accesses, helping developers pinpoint and resolve race conditions.

Best Practices for Debugging

When debugging applications that utilize goroutines, it's advisable
to start with a high-level runtime analysis using runtime.Stack or
profiling with pprof to gain an overview of the application's state.
Following this, more focused techniques, such as enabling the race
detector, can be applied to identify and resolve specific issues. Additionally, incorporating structured logging at key execution points in
goroutines can provide further insights into the application's behavior.

By combining these tools and methodologies, developers can effectively tackle the complexities of debugging concurrent applications
in Go.

2.11   Real-world Examples of Goroutines

In concurrent programming in Go, goroutines stand as a cornerstone feature, enabling the development of high-performance, scalable applications. This section will illustrate the utility of goroutines through a series of real-world examples, showcasing their effectiveness in various scenarios.

Web Server Handling Concurrent Requests

A common application of goroutines is in the development of web servers that can handle multiple requests concurrently. Below is an example demonstrating how a simple web server in Go can utilize goroutines to manage incoming HTTP requests.

```
1   package main
2
3   import (
4       "fmt"
5       "net/http"
6   )
7
8   func handler(w http.ResponseWriter, r *http.Request) {
9       fmt.Fprintf(w, "Hello, %s!", r.URL.Path[1:])
10  }
11
12  func main() {
13      http.HandleFunc("/", handler)
14      fmt.Println("Starting server on :8080")
15      http.ListenAndServe(":8080", nil)
16  }
```

In this example, the http.HandleFunc function routes incoming requests to the handler function. When http.ListenAndServe is called, the server starts listening on port 8080. For each incoming request, the Go runtime creates a new goroutine where the handler function runs, allowing the server to handle multiple requests concurrently without blocking.

Concurrent Processing of Data

Goroutines are also highly effective for tasks requiring concurrent processing of data. Consider a scenario where we have a slice of URLs and the task is to fetch and process data from these URLs concurrently. Below is a simplified example:

```
 1  package main
 2
 3  import (
 4      "fmt"
 5      "net/http"
 6      "sync"
 7  )
 8
 9  func fetchURL(wg *sync.WaitGroup, url string) {
10      defer wg.Done()
11      resp, err := http.Get(url)
12      if err != nil {
13          fmt.Println(err)
14          return
15      }
16      fmt.Printf("%s responded with status code: %d\n", url, resp.StatusCode)
17  }
18
19  func main() {
20      urls := []string{
21          "http://example.com",
22          "http://example.net",
23          // Add more URLs as necessary
24      }
25      var wg sync.WaitGroup
26      wg.Add(len(urls))
27
28      for _, url := range urls {
29          go fetchURL(&wg, url)
30      }
31
32      wg.Wait()
33  }
```

In this code, fetchURL is designed to fetch data from a given URL, and it's invoked as a goroutine for each URL in the slice. The sync.WaitGroup is employed to ensure that the main goroutine waits for all the fetch goroutines to complete before exiting.

Fan-out, Fan-in Pattern for Data Aggregation

The fan-out, fan-in pattern is a powerful concurrency pattern facilitated by goroutines, allowing parallel execution of tasks and aggregation of results. Here's how it can be implemented in Go:

```go
package main

import (
    "fmt"
    "sync"
)

func worker(id int, jobs <-chan int, results chan<- int) {
    for job := range jobs {
        fmt.Printf("worker %d started job %d\n", id, job)
        results <- job * 2 // Example processing
        fmt.Printf("worker %d finished job %d\n", id, job)
    }
}

func main() {
    jobs := make(chan int, 100)
    results := make(chan int, 100)

    // Start 3 workers.
    for w := 1; w <= 3; w++ {
        go worker(w, jobs, results)
    }

    // Sending 9 jobs and then closing the channel to indicate that's all the
        work we have.
    for j := 1; j <= 9; j++ {
        jobs <- j
    }
    close(jobs)

    // Finally, collect all the results of the work.
    for a := 1; a <= 9; a++ {
        <-results
    }
}
```

This pattern utilizes two channels: 'jobs' for distributing work
among workers and 'results' for collecting the outcomes. Each
'worker' goroutine processes jobs from the 'jobs' channel and sends
the result to the 'results' channel. The main function oversees
distributing jobs and gathering results, demonstrating an effective
way to manage parallel processing in Go.

These examples underline the versatility of goroutines in Go, showcasing their capability to enhance application performance through concurrent execution. Whether serving high volumes of web requests, processing data in parallel, or employing concurrency patterns like fan-out, fan-in, goroutines offer a straightforward yet powerful solution for leveraging the capabilities of modern multi-core processors.

2.12   Advanced Goroutine Patterns

Advanced goroutine patterns in Go programming are essential for developers aiming to harness the full potential of concurrency in their applications. This section will explore several sophisticated patterns, including worker pools, pipelines, and rate limiting. Each of these patterns addresses different aspects of concurrent programming and offers solutions to common challenges such as workload distribution, data processing sequences, and controlling the rate of operation execution.

Worker Pools

Worker pools are a concurrency pattern used to limit the number of goroutines running concurrently, based on a predefined set of workers. This pattern is particularly useful for controlling resources and ensuring that a system does not become overwhelmed by too many concurrent operations.

```
// Example of a worker pool in Go
package main

import (
    "fmt"
    "sync"
    "time"
)

func worker(id int, jobs <-chan int, results chan<- int) {
    for j := range jobs {
        fmt.Println("worker", id, "processing job", j)
        time.Sleep(time.Second)
        results <- j * 2
    }
```

```
16   }
17
18   func main() {
19       jobs := make(chan int, 100)
20       results := make(chan int, 100)
21
22       // Create 3 workers
23       for w := 1; w <= 3; w++ {
24           go worker(w, jobs, results)
25       }
26
27       // Sending 9 jobs
28       for j := 1; j <= 9; j++ {
29           jobs <- j
30       }
31       close(jobs)
32
33       // Receiving results
34       for a := 1; a <= 9; a++ {
35           <-results
36       }
37   }
```

The above example demonstrates a simple worker pool where 3 workers process 9 jobs. Each worker receives jobs from the jobs channel, processes the job (simulated by sleeping for a second), and sends the result to the results channel.

Pipelines

Pipelines are a pattern for connecting multiple goroutines together so that the output of one is the input to another. This pattern is useful for processing streams or sequences of data.

```
1    // Example of a pipeline in Go
2    package main
3
4    import "fmt"
5
6    func generate(nums ...int) <-chan int {
7        out := make(chan int)
8        go func() {
9            for _, n := range nums {
10               out <- n
11           }
12           close(out)
13       }()
14       return out
15   }
16
```

```
17   func square(in <-chan int) <-chan int {
18       out := make(chan int)
19       go func() {
20           for n := range in {
21               out <- n * n
22           }
23           close(out)
24       }()
25       return out
26   }
27
28   func main() {
29       // Set up the pipeline.
30       nums := generate(2, 3)
31       out := square(nums)
32
33       // Consume the output.
34       fmt.Println(<-out) // 4
35       fmt.Println(<-out) // 9
36   }
```

In this pipeline example, numbers are generated and then squared.
The 'generate' function sends numbers to be processed, and the
'square' function receives numbers, squares them, and passes them
on.

Rate Limiting

Rate limiting is crucial for controlling the rate of operations to avoid
overwhelming resources or exceeding API usage quotas. In Go, a
common approach to rate limiting is using a ticker.

```
1    // Example of rate limiting in Go
2    package main
3
4    import (
5        "fmt"
6        "time"
7    )
8
9    func main() {
10       requests := make(chan int, 5)
11       for i := 1; i <= 5; i++ {
12           requests <- i
13       }
14       close(requests)
15
16       limiter := time.Tick(200 * time.Millisecond)
17
18       for req := range requests {
```

```
19        <-limiter
20        fmt.Println("request", req, time.Now())
21    }
22 }
```

This example demonstrates limiting the handling of requests to one every 200 milliseconds, using a ticker.

By utilizing advanced goroutine patterns such as worker pools, pipelines, and rate limiting, Go developers can write more efficient, robust, and scalable concurrent applications. Each pattern serves a different purpose and can be used in combination to solve complex concurrency problems.

Chapter 3

Channels in Go: Communication between Goroutines

Channels are a powerful feature in Go that facilitate communication and synchronization between goroutines, enabling the development of complex concurrent patterns without the common pitfalls of other concurrency mechanisms, such as deadlocks or race conditions. They act as conduits through which goroutines can send and receive values, ensuring safe and synchronized data exchange. This chapter explores the various types of channels, their syntax, and practical applications, along with advanced techniques for channel-based communication. Through comprehending channels, developers can architect robust and efficient concurrent applications in Go.

3.1   Introduction to Channels

Channels in Go provide a powerful mechanism for concurrent programming by facilitating communication between goroutines. They serve as conduits through which goroutines can send and receive values, effectively maintaining synchronized data exchange and ensuring safe communication. This capability is crucial for developing applications that require high levels of concurrency without falling into common traps associated with parallel execution, such as deadlocks and race conditions.

At its core, a channel is typified by the nature of data it transports, denoted in its declaration. To illustrate, a channel that transfers integers is declared differently from one that handles strings. This strong typing enhances code safety and clarity. The declaration syntax for a channel transporting integers is as follows:

```
1   var channelName chan int
```

This line declares a variable channelName as a channel for 'int' type data. It's important to note that this channel is 'nil' by default, meaning it must be initialized before use, which can be achieved using the built-in 'make' function:

```
1   channelName = make(chan int)
```

One of the quintessential operations on channels is sending and receiving data, which is achieved using the channel operator <-. For sending data to the channel:

```
1   channelName <- 10
```

This line sends the integer '10' through channelName. Conversely, to receive data from the channel and assign it to a variable:

```
1   value := <-channelName
```

At this juncture, value will hold the integer that was sent through the channel. These operations are blocking by nature; a send operation on a channel will block the goroutine until another goroutine reads from the channel, and vice versa. This behavior is foundational to achieving synchronization between goroutines, as it ensures that data is fully transferred before the receiving goroutine proceeds with its execution.

The mechanism of channels extends beyond simple data exchange. It encompasses complex patterns of concurrent communication, such as signaling the completion of tasks, distributing work among multiple goroutines, and aggregating results from parallel operations. Channels, therefore, are not merely a feature of Go's concurrency model but are fundamental to architecting sophisticated and efficient concurrent applications.

Understanding channels and their correct application is essential for leveraging Go's full potential in developing concurrent applications. The subsequent sections will delve deeper into channel types, operations, and patterns, providing the foundational knowledge and practical insights needed to master concurrent programming with Go.

3.2   Creating and Using Channels

Channels in Go are a core part of its concurrency model and are especially designed to enable goroutines to communicate with each other safely. This section elucidates the process of creating and utilizing channels, which is integral for employing Go's concurrent programming capabilities effectively.

To begin, creating a channel in Go is accomplished using the built-in make function. The syntax for creating a channel is quite straightforward:

```
1  ch := make(chan Type)
```

Here, Type specifies the type of values that the channel is allowed to transport. It can be an integer, string, or even a struct. The type declaration ensures type safety, meaning that the channel can only be used to send and receive values of the specified type.

Channels can be both bidirectional and unidirectional depending on the requirements. By default, a channel is bidirectional, which means it can be used to both send and receive messages. However, it is possible to declare a channel as send-only or receive-only by specifying the direction at the time of its declaration:

```
1   sendOnly := make(chan<- int)
2   receiveOnly := make(<-chan int)
```

In the above declarations, sendOnly can only be used to send integers, and receiveOnly can only be used to receive integers. This specification can enhance the clarity and safety of the code by clearly indicating the intention of use.

To send a value into a channel, the <- operator is used:

```
1   ch <- value
```

Receiving a value from a channel is also performed with the <- operator, but on the other side of the channel variable:

```
1   value := <-ch
```

It's important to understand that both send and receive operations are blocking by nature. When a goroutine tries to send data on a channel, it will block until another goroutine receives that data from the channel. Similarly, a goroutine that tries to receive data from a channel will block until data is sent on that channel.

One of the common practices with channels is to use them within a select statement to implement non-blocking send or receive operations. By using a default case, the select statement can proceed without blocking if no other case is ready:

```
1   select {
2   case ch <- value:
3       // the value was successfully sent
4   default:
5       // the send operation would block, so we do something else
6   }
```

Similarly, for receiving:

```
1   select {
2   case value := <-ch:
3       // received a value from the channel
```

```
4  default:
5      // the receive operation would block, so we do something else
6  }
```

This mechanism is particularly useful when dealing with multiple channels or when ensuring that a goroutine does not get indefinitely blocked waiting on a channel operation.

Closing a channel is achieved using the close function. It is a critical operation that signals no more values will be sent on the channel. However, it is still possible to receive values from a closed channel if the channel is buffered and elements are present in the buffer. Attempting to send a value on a closed channel will result in a runtime panic, underscoring the importance of coordinating channel operations carefully.

```
1  close(ch)
```

To summarize, understanding and applying the concepts of creating and using channels are fundamental for developing concurrent applications in Go. Proper usage of channels enables safe and synchronized communication between goroutines, thereby empowering developers to build more robust and efficient applications.

3.3 Types of Channels: Unbuffered and Buffered

In Go, channels are typed conduits that allow the transmission of values between goroutines. These channels can be classified into two main types: unbuffered and buffered. Understanding the distinction between these two types is crucial for designing effective concurrent programs.

Unbuffered Channels

Unbuffered channels are the most direct form of channel communication. When a value is sent on an unbuffered channel, the sending goroutine is blocked until another goroutine is ready to receive the value. Conversely, if a goroutine attempts to receive a value off an unbuffered channel, it will block until a value is sent. This ensures that both send and receive operations are synchronized, allowing goroutines to coordinate with precision. The syntax for creating an unbuffered channel for transmitting values of type int is shown below:

```
1   ch := make(chan int)
```

An example demonstrating a basic send and receive operation with an unbuffered channel is as follows:

```
1   package main
2
3   import (
4       "fmt"
5   )
6
7   func main() {
8       ch := make(chan int)
9
10      go func() {
11          ch <- 42 // Sending value to channel
12      }()
13
14      val := <-ch // Receiving value from channel
15      fmt.Println(val)
16  }
```

The output of this program would unambiguously be:

42

Buffered Channels

Buffered channels, on the other hand, introduce a capacity to the channel, allowing values to be sent to the channel without immediately requiring a corresponding receive operation. This capacity enables the channel to store values temporarily until they are explicitly received. If the channel's buffer is full, any attempt to send more values will block until there is space available. Similarly, if the buffer is empty, a receive operation will block until a value is sent to the channel. The syntax for creating a buffered channel for

74

int values with a buffer size of n is as follows:

```
1   ch := make(chan int, n)
```

Consider the following example that illustrates the use of a buffered channel:

```
1    package main
2
3    import (
4        "fmt"
5    )
6
7    func main() {
8        ch := make(chan int, 2) // Creating a buffered channel with a capacity of 2
9
10       // Sending values to channel without immediate receipt
11       ch <- 42
12       ch <- 27
13
14       fmt.Println(<-ch) // Receiving values from channel
15       fmt.Println(<-ch)
16   }
```

This would produce the output:

```
42
27
```

It's important to note that even buffered channels can become blocked if the buffer is either full during send operations or empty during receive operations. The judicious use of buffered channels can significantly enhance the performance and responsiveness of a Go application by allowing goroutines to proceed with their execution without waiting for immediate synchronization with other goroutines.

In summary, understanding the operational semantics and implications of unbuffered and buffered channels is foundational to employing channels effectively within concurrent Go applications. This comprehension enables developers to choose the appropriate type of channel and buffer size based on the specific requirements and expected behaviors of the application's concurrent components.

3.4   Sending and Receiving: The Basics of Channel Communication

Channels in Go serve as pipelines through which goroutines exchange data. To harness the full potential of channels, an essential grasp of sending and receiving data is paramount. This functionality is built into Go's syntax and design, providing a straightforward yet powerful way to synchronize the execution of goroutines.

When a channel is created, it is associated with a specific type, which determines the kind of data that can be transmitted through the channel. This type-specific nature ensures type safety, preventing common programming errors that could occur when dealing with concurrent data exchange.

Sending Data to a Channel

To send data to a channel, the syntax utilizes the channel variable followed by the arrow operator ($\leftarrow$) and then the data to be sent. The operation blocks until another goroutine is ready to receive the data, ensuring that the send operation is safely synchronized.

Consider the following example showcasing the send operation:

```
1  ch := make(chan int) // Creating a new channel of integers
2  go func() {
3      ch <- 42 // Sending an integer to the channel
4  }()
```

In this example, a goroutine is spawned to send the value 42 to the ch channel. The send operation will wait until another goroutine performs a receive operation on the ch channel.

Receiving Data from a Channel

Receiving data from a channel is as straightforward as sending data. The syntax also uses the arrow operator ($\leftarrow$), but in this case, it points towards the channel variable. This operation blocks until data is available to be received, ensuring that the receive operation is synchronized with a corresponding send operation.

Following is an example of the receive operation:

```
1  value := <-ch // Receiving data from the channel
```

This statement halts execution until an integer is sent to the ch channel, after which it assigns the received value to the value variable.

The Role of Blocking in Synchronization

Both sending and receiving operations are blocking by nature. This is a fundamental aspect of how channels ensure data synchronization between goroutines. When an operation blocks, it does so until the corresponding send or receive action is performed on the other end of the channel.

This blocking behavior is illustrated below:

```
Sending goroutine: Blocked until receive operation occurs
Receiving goroutine: Blocked until send operation provides data
```

The mechanism of blocking until the complementary operation is ready ensures that data is not lost and that both operations are synchronized. This prevents race conditions and enhances the reliability of concurrent Go programs.

Understanding the basics of sending and receiving data with channels is foundational to mastering concurrent programming in Go. By leveraging these operations and their inherent synchronization capabilities, developers can architect more robust and efficient concurrent applications.

3.5   Closing Channels and Handling Closed Channels

Closing a channel in Go indicates that no more values will be sent on it. This is a critical concept in asynchronous programming with Go as it provides a way to signal the receivers that the channel's lifecycle has come to an end. To close a channel, the close function is used. It's important to note that only the sender should close a channel, and never the receiver. Closing an already closed channel or attempting to send a value on a closed channel will result in a runtime panic.

```
1   close(ch)
```

After a channel is closed, it's still possible to receive values from the channel. If there are remaining values in the channel, they can be received until the channel is empty. Once empty, any receive operation on the channel will immediately return the zero value for the channel's type without blocking.

```
1   v, ok := <-ch
```

In the above statement, v will receive the value from the channel ch. The second value, ok, is a boolean that is true if the received value was sent on the channel before the channel was closed, and false if the value was received because the channel was closed and empty.

Handling closed channels properly is paramount to avoid deadlocks and ensure the correct flow of information. A common pattern for receiving from a channel until it's closed involves using a for loop and the range keyword.

```
1   for v := range ch {
2       // Process v
3   }
```

This loop automatically breaks when the channel ch is closed, and there are no more values to receive, making it a convenient and safe way to consume channel data.

However, there are situations where the sender may not have the knowledge of when to close the channel, or multiple goroutines are sending to the channel, and coordination is necessary to decide when to close it safely. In such cases, it's essential to design the application to ensure there's a clear ownership of channel closure, often by dedicating a single goroutine to closing the channel under the correct conditions.

One of the common mistakes in using channels is closing them too early or when there are still potential senders. This can cause program panics due to sending on a closed channel. A solution is to use synchronization techniques, such as wait groups or other channels, to signal when it's safe to close a channel.

Closing channels and correctly handling them is instrumental in leveraging Go's concurrency features effectively. Through practice and understanding the nuances involved in channel communication, developers can avoid common pitfalls and harness the power of Go's channels to build responsive and concurrent applications.

3.6 Range Loops with Channels

Channels in Go provide a robust mechanism for goroutines to communicate effectively, ensuring that data is transferred safely between concurrently running parts of an application. One powerful construct for consuming data from channels is the use of range loops. This section delineates the utilization of range loops with channels, their syntax, and practical examples to guide developers in implementing these constructs in their Go applications.

Range loops offer a convenient and clear syntax for iterating over the items sent through a channel. By leveraging a range loop with a channel, a goroutine can continuously receive values sent to the channel until it is closed.

The basic syntax for using a range loop with a channel is as follows:

```
1  for value := range channel {
```

```
2        // Process value
3    }
```

In this construct, channel is the channel from which values are received, and value is the variable that each item received from the channel will be assigned to within the loop. It is crucial to note that the range loop will continue to receive values from the channel until the channel is closed. If the channel is not closed, the range loop will block, waiting for new values, and lead to a deadlock situation if no values are forthcoming.

A practical example of using range loops with an unbuffered channel is as follows:

```
1    package main
2
3    import (
4        "fmt"
5    )
6
7    func main() {
8        // Create an unbuffered channel of integers
9        messages := make(chan int)
10
11       // Launch a goroutine to send values to the channel
12       go func() {
13           for i := 0; i < 5; i++ {
14               messages <- i
15           }
16           close(messages) // Important: closing the channel
17       }()
18
19       // Use range loop to receive values from the channel
20       for message := range messages {
21           fmt.Println(message)
22       }
23   }
```

The code above demonstrates creating an unbuffered integer channel, messages, and a goroutine that sends integers 0 through 4 to this channel. Once all values are sent, the channel is closed using close(messages). In the main goroutine, a range loop iterates over each value received from the messages channel, printing it to the console. The output of the program will be:

```
0
1
2
```

3
4

It is imperative to close the channel once all values have been sent to prevent the range loop from blocking indefinitely. Closing a channel signals that no more values will be sent on it, allowing the range loop to terminate after receiving all sent values.

This example underscores the importance of closing channels when they are no longer needed to avoid goroutine leaks and ensure clean and efficient control flow in concurrent applications.

Range loops with channels in Go are an elegant and idiomatic way to process streams of data communicated between goroutines. This construct simplifies the handling of concurrent data transfer, making Go a powerful language for developing sophisticated concurrent applications.

3.7 Select and Default Case for Channels

The select statement in Go offers a sophisticated mechanism for goroutines to interact concurrently with multiple channels. It permits a goroutine to wait on multiple communication operations, progressing with one that is ready to execute. The default case in a select statement, meanwhile, enables the execution of non-blocking operations, ensuring that a goroutine doesn't remain indefinitely idle if no channels are ready for communication.

The syntax for a select statement encompasses multiple cases, each corresponding to a communication operation - either sending or receiving. When none of the cases can proceed because the channels are not ready (either full for send operations or empty for receive operations), the select statement blocks. However, if a default case is present, the select will execute this default case immediately, facilitating non-blocking channel operations.

To understand the select statement's usage, consider the following example where a goroutine waits on two channels:

```
1   func process(ch1, ch2 <-chan int) {
```

```
2    select {
3    case v := <-ch1:
4        fmt.Println("Received from ch1:", v)
5    case v := <-ch2:
6        fmt.Println("Received from ch2:", v)
7    default:
8        fmt.Println("No data received from channels.")
9    }
10   }
```

In this example, the function process waits for data from either ch1 or ch2. The select statement first checks if any of the cases is ready to proceed. If ch1 or ch2 has data ready to be received, the corresponding case executes. If neither channel is ready, the default case is executed, outputting "No data received from channels."

The incorporation of the default case is crucial for preventing goroutines from blocking indefinitely, especially in scenarios where channels might not be ready to communicate within a specific timeframe. This is particularly useful for implementing timeouts or polling mechanisms without resorting to additional goroutines or complicated synchronization logic.

The select statement's versatility is further highlighted when employed in a loop, offering a robust pattern for handling multiple channels dynamically. For example, the following code snippet demonstrates how to use the select statement within a loop to continuously process data from two channels until both are closed:

```
1    for {
2        select {
3        case v, ok := <-ch1:
4            if !ok {
5                ch1 = nil
6                continue
7            }
8            fmt.Println("Received from ch1:", v)
9        case v, ok := <-ch2:
10           if !ok {
11               ch2 = nil
12               continue
13           }
14           fmt.Println("Received from ch2:", v)
15       default:
16           fmt.Println("Waiting for data...")
17           time.Sleep(100 * time.Millisecond)
18       }
19       if ch1 == nil && ch2 == nil {
```

```
20        break
21    }
22  }
```

In this scenario, the loop continues as long as there is a potential for receiving data from either ch1 or ch2. When a channel is closed, and no more data can be received, its corresponding variable is set to nil, rendering its case inoperative in subsequent select iterations. This pattern ensures that the function gracefully terminates once all channels have been adequately processed.

The select statement, especially when combined with the default case, thus serves as a cornerstone for building responsive, non-blocking concurrent applications in Go. It enables developers to efficiently manage multiple channels within a single goroutine, simplifying the architecture of concurrent systems and enhancing their scalability and maintainability.

3.8 Deadlocks and How to Avoid Them

Deadlocks occur in concurrent programming when two or more goroutines are blocked forever, each waiting for another to release a lock. In the context of Go using channels, deadlocks happen when goroutines attempt to perform operations on channels without corresponding senders or receivers. The danger of deadlocks cannot be overstated as they halt the execution of a program, wasting computational resources and complicating debugging and troubleshooting processes. To mitigate the risk of deadlocks, developers must understand their causes and implement strategies to prevent them.

The first step in avoiding deadlocks is to ensure that every send operation on a channel has a corresponding receive operation, and vice versa. This symmetry is crucial for preventing goroutines from being indefinitely blocked. The following example demonstrates a simple scenario where a deadlock might occur:

```
1  func main() {
2      ch := make(chan int)
```

```
3
4    go func() {
5        ch <- 1 // Sending operation
6    }()
7
8    // Missing a receive operation here can lead to a deadlock
9  }
```

In the example above, a goroutine is created to send a value into the channel, but there is no corresponding receive operation. If the main goroutine does not include a receive operation for the value sent on the channel, the program will deadlock since the sending goroutine will block indefinitely waiting for its value to be received.

To avoid such deadlocks, ensure that the main goroutine or another goroutine is always ready to receive the sent value, as shown below:

```
1  func main() {
2      ch := make(chan int)
3
4      go func() {
5          ch <- 1 // Sending operation
6      }()
7
8      value := <-ch // Receive operation
9      fmt.Println(value)
10 }
```

Another strategy for preventing deadlocks involves the use of buffered channels. Buffered channels allow a certain number of values to be sent without a corresponding receive operation, up to the capacity of the buffer. This capacity can provide the necessary flexibility to prevent goroutines from blocking when there is a temporary mismatch in the number of send and receive operations. However, developers must use buffered channels judiciously, as mismanagement of buffer sizes can still lead to deadlocks if the buffer becomes full and no further sends can proceed without a receive.

Consider the following example that utilizes a buffered channel:

```
1  func main() {
2      ch := make(chan int, 1) // Creating a buffered channel with a capacity of 1
3
4      go func() {
5          ch <- 1 // This send operation is non-blocking due to the buffer
6      }()
```

```
 7
 8      value := <-ch // Receive operation
 9      fmt.Println(value)
10    }
```

In this instance, the send operation inside the goroutine does not block even if there is no immediate receive operation, thanks to the buffer in the channel. The program can proceed smoothly and avoid a deadlock.

A more advanced strategy to avoid deadlocks involves the `select` statement with a `default` clause, which allows a non-blocking send or receive operation. The `select` statement enables a goroutine to attempt an operation on a channel but proceed without blocking if the operation cannot be immediately performed.

Understanding and preventing deadlocks requires careful attention to the design of concurrent programs. Developers must ensure a balance between send and receive operations on channels, consider the use of buffered channels where appropriate, and utilize the `select` statement with a `default` clause to prevent goroutines from blocking indefinitely. By adhering to these practices, programmers can mitigate the risk of deadlocks and develop efficient, reliable concurrent applications in Go.

3.9 Channel Patterns: Fan-in and Fan-out

Channels in Go not only facilitate communication between goroutines but also enable implementation of advanced concurrency patterns. Two such patterns are Fan-in and Fan-out, which are instrumental in improving the efficiency of data handling and processing across multiple goroutines. These patterns are particularly useful in scenarios involving tasks like data aggregation from multiple sources and distributing tasks among multiple workers for parallel processing.

Fan-out

The Fan-out pattern involves starting multiple goroutines to handle tasks concurrently, thereby distributing work across system resources. This pattern is typically used to speed up processing by parallelizing work.

Consider an example where we need to process a large set of data points. By employing the Fan-out pattern, each data point can be processed in parallel, significantly reducing overall processing time.

```
func processData(points []Data) {
    numWorkers := 5
    tasks := make(chan Data, len(points))
    // Fan-out
    for i := 0; i < numWorkers; i++ {
        go func() {
            for task := range tasks {
                process(task)
            }
        }()
    }
    for _, point := range points {
        tasks <- point
    }
    close(tasks)
}
```

In this example, numWorkers goroutines are created, each reading from the tasks channel. Data points are sent into the tasks channel, and each worker picks up a task and processes it. This exemplifies the Fan-out pattern by distributing tasks among multiple workers.

Fan-in

The Fan-in pattern is the inverse of Fan-out. It involves combining multiple results into a single channel. This is particularly useful for aggregating results from multiple sources.

Here is an example that demonstrates the Fan-in pattern. It involves collecting results from multiple workers into a single channel for further processing.

```
func collect(results ...<-chan Result) <-chan Result {
    var wg sync.WaitGroup
```

```
3     merged := make(chan Result)
4
5     output := func(c <-chan Result) {
6         for result := range c {
7             merged <- result
8         }
9         wg.Done()
10    }
11
12    wg.Add(len(results))
13    for _, resultChannel := range results {
14        go output(resultChannel)
15    }
16
17    go func() {
18        wg.Wait()
19        close(merged)
20    }()
21
22    return merged
23  }
```

In this `collect` function, results from multiple channels are merged into the `merged` channel. This is achieved by launching a goroutine for each input channel that forwards its results to `merged`. The use of a `WaitGroup` ensures that all forwarding goroutines complete before `merged` is closed, which exemplifies the Fan-in pattern.

Combining Fan-in and Fan-out

Combining Fan-in and Fan-out patterns can be highly effective in scenarios where tasks need to be distributed among workers for processing, and their results subsequently aggregated. This combination embodies a powerful concurrency model that leverages Go's channels and goroutines to achieve high performance and efficient data processing.

To summarize, Fan-out and Fan-in patterns stand as pillars for concurrent programming in Go, enabling developers to efficiently distribute tasks and aggregate results. Through these patterns, Go's concurrency primitives can be utilized to their fullest potential, paving the way for highly concurrent and responsive applications.

This section details the implementation and use of the Fan-in and Fan-out patterns in Go, providing clear examples and explanations on how to leverage these patterns for efficient concurrent programming.

3.10   Using Channels for Signaling

Channels in Go not only serve the purpose of data exchange between goroutines but also play a crucial role in signaling mechanisms. This can range from notifying goroutines to start processing, to signaling termination or readiness. Signaling via channels enhances the control flow in concurrent Go programs, ensuring that goroutines operate in a coordinated manner.

Signaling with Empty Structs

One common pattern for signaling between goroutines involves using channels of type struct{}. An empty struct in Go does not consume memory, making it an ideal candidate for signaling without transferring data.

```
done := make(chan struct{})

go func() {
    // Perform some work
    ...
    // Signal completion
    close(done)
}()

<-done // Wait for signal
```

Here, the channel done is closed to signal that a particular operation has completed. The receiving goroutine blocks until it receives this signal. Using an empty struct emphasizes that the value is irrelevant—only the act of sending a signal matters.

Boolean Channels for State Signaling

Alternatively, a channel of type bool can indicate the completion of an operation with more context—such as whether the operation was successful.

```
1   success := make(chan bool)
2
3   go func() {
4       // Attempt an operation
5       result := performOperation()
6       // Signal success or failure
7       success <- result
8   }()
9
10  if <-success {
11      fmt.Println("Operation succeeded")
12  } else {
13      fmt.Println("Operation failed")
14  }
```

The boolean value sent through the channel success provides additional information about the operation's outcome, enabling the receiving goroutine to adjust its flow accordingly.

Channels for Timeout Signaling

Time-sensitive operations can leverage channels alongside the time.After function to implement timeouts. This pattern prevents goroutines from waiting indefinitely, enhancing the robustness of concurrent applications.

```
1   result := make(chan Type) // Type represents the operation's result type
2   timeout := time.After(5 * time.Second)
3
4   go func() {
5       // Perform operation and send result
6       result <- performOperation()
7   }()
8
9   select {
10  case res := <-result:
11      fmt.Println("Received result:", res)
12  case <-timeout:
13      fmt.Println("Operation timed out")
14  }
```

The select statement waits on multiple channel operations, handling them as soon as one unblocks. If the operation completes within the timeout, its result is processed. Otherwise, the timeout case is selected, allowing the program to proceed without the operation's result.

Implementing Condition Variables with Channels

Channels can be used to implement condition variables, synchronizing the execution flow based on certain conditions.

```
1   var mutex = &sync.Mutex{}
2   cond := sync.NewCond(mutex)
3
4   ready := make(chan bool)
5
6   go func() {
7       mutex.Lock()
8       for !condition() {
9           cond.Wait()
10      }
11      mutex.Unlock()
12      ready <- true
13  }()
```

This example leverages channels in conjunction with condition variables from the sync package. Here, a goroutine waits for a condition to become true, using cond.Wait(). Once the condition is met, it signals another goroutine via the ready channel.

By utilizing channels for signaling, Go developers can implement sophisticated concurrency patterns with greater control over goroutine execution. Whether it's coordinating start and stop signals, implementing timeouts, or synchronizing state, channels provide a versatile mechanism for managing concurrency.

3.11   Timeouts and Canceling with Channels

Interactions with channels in Go can potentially block execution indefinitely, especially when a read is attempted from an empty channel or a write is attempted on a channel with no available buffer space. In real-world applications, allowing goroutines to block indefinitely is often undesirable, potentially leading to deadlocks or wasted system resources. To manage these situations, Go provides mechanisms for implementing timeouts and cancellation signals using channels, thereby offering more control over goroutine execution.

Implementing Timeouts

Timeouts are critical in preventing a goroutine from waiting on a channel operation indefinitely. They are implemented using Go's time package, specifically the time.After function, which returns a chan that sends the current time after a specified duration.

Consider a scenario where you have a worker goroutine performing a task that might hang or take longer than expected. To avoid blocking the entire program, you can implement a timeout as follows:

```
package main

import (
    "fmt"
    "time"
)

func main() {
    workChan := make(chan bool)

    go func() {
        time.Sleep(2 * time.Second) // Simulate work
        workChan <- true
    }()

    select {
    case <-workChan:
        fmt.Println("Work completed successfully.")
    case <-time.After(1 * time.Second):
        fmt.Println("Work timed out.")
    }
}
```

In the example above, the select statement is used to wait on multiple channel operations. The first case listens for a completion signal from workChan, while the second case listens for a timeout signal from time.After. If the work takes longer than the specified timeout duration, the program will print "Work timed out." instead of hanging indefinitely.

Canceling with Channels

In addition to timeouts, channels can also be used to signal cancellation of ongoing tasks. This is particularly useful when you want to abort a task that no longer needs to be completed. A common approach is to use a dedicated cancellation channel on which a signal can be sent to indicate that the work should be stopped.

Here's how you can implement a cancellable task:

```go
package main

import (
    "fmt"
    "time"
)

func performTask(cancelChan chan struct{}) {
    for {
        select {
        case <-cancelChan:
            fmt.Println("Task was cancelled.")
            return
        default:
            // Perform some unit of work
            time.Sleep(500 * time.Millisecond) // Simulate work
        }
    }
}

func main() {
    cancelChan := make(chan struct{})

    go performTask(cancelChan)

    // Simulate task cancellation after 2 seconds
    time.Sleep(2 * time.Second)
    close(cancelChan)
}
```

In this example, performTask checks for a cancellation signal by listening on cancelChan. The main goroutine sleeps for a certain duration (simulating other work) before closing cancelChan, signaling performTask to stop execution. By closing the channel rather than sending a specific value, we ensure that all receivers of the channel receive the signal immediately, making it an effective way to broadcast a cancellation event.

Through the judicious use of timeouts and cancellation channels, developers can write more robust, responsive Go programs that handle long-running or potentially-hanging operations gracefully. These patterns are essential components in the development of concurrent applications, allowing for more precise control over goroutine execution flow and resource management.

3.12 Advanced Channel Techniques and Patterns

In concurrent programming within Go, channels serve as the cornerstone for facilitating communication and synchronization amongst goroutines. This section elucidates upon the more intricate channel techniques and patterns, empowering developers with the knowledge to unlock the full potential of concurrent application architecture.

Multiplexing with Channels

Central to advanced usage of channels is the concept of multiplexing, where a single channel is used to handle data from multiple sources. This pattern enhances the efficiency of data handling, reducing the overhead associated with managing multiple channels simultaneously.

To implement channel multiplexing, a select statement is utilized within a loop. Consider the following example where data from two channels is processed through a single select statement:

```
1  func multiplex(channel1, channel2 <-chan int) <-chan int {
2      output := make(chan int)
3      go func() {
4          for {
5              select {
6              case msg1 := <-channel1:
7                  output <- msg1
8              case msg2 := <-channel2:
9                  output <- msg2
10             }
11         }
12     }()
```

```
13      return output
14  }
```

The select statement blocks until one of its cases can proceed, effectively multiplexing the inputs from channel1 and channel2 into the output channel.

Channel Factories

Channel factories are functions that encapsulate the creation and return of a channel. This pattern is remarkably useful for abstracting channel setup and management, especially when dealing with asynchronous data streams.

Consider the function below that returns a channel through which it sends a sequence of numbers:

```
1   func numberGenerator(start, end int) <-chan int {
2       channel := make(chan int)
3       go func() {
4           for i := start; i <= end; i++ {
5               channel <- i
6           }
7           close(channel)
8       }()
9       return channel
10  }
```

The returned channel can then be consumed using a range loop, abstracting away the goroutine management details from the caller.

Timeouts using select

A common challenge in concurrent operations is preventing goroutines from waiting indefinitely on channel operations. The Go programming language addresses this challenge through the use of the select statement with a time.After case, enabling the implementation of timeouts.

The following snippet demarcates a timeout operation where a channel read operation is given a one-second timeout:

```go
func readWithTimeout(channel <-chan int) (int, bool) {
    select {
    case msg := <-channel:
        return msg, true
    case <-time.After(1 * time.Second):
        return 0, false
    }
}
```

If the channel does not receive any data within one second, time.After sends the current time on its channel, triggering the timeout case.

Using Channels as Futures

In concurrent programming, a future represents a value that may become available at some point. Channels in Go can be employed to implement this pattern, providing an elegant way to handle asynchronous computations.

Consider the implementation of a simple future using a channel:

```go
func computeFuture(value int) <-chan int {
    future := make(chan int)
    go func() {
        // Simulate a computation
        time.Sleep(1 * time.Second)
        future <- value * 2
    }()
    return future
}
```

The computeFuture function initiates a computation in a new goroutine, immediately returning a channel through which the result will be sent. This pattern allows other parts of the application to proceed without blocking, later synchronizing on the result.

Equipped with these advanced techniques and patterns, developers can adeptly enhance the responsiveness and performance of their Go applications, leveraging channels to their utmost potential.

Chapter 4

Synchronization Primitives: Mutexes and Cond

In concurrent programming, ensuring that only one goroutine accesses a variable at a time is crucial for preventing data races and ensuring thread safety. Go's standard library provides synchronization primitives such as Mutexes and Cond to facilitate this. Mutexes ensure that resources are accessed in a mutually exclusive manner, while Condition Variables (Cond) allow goroutines to wait for or signal specific conditions. This chapter offers an in-depth look at these primitives, demonstrating their usage through examples and highlighting best practices for achieving synchronization in Go applications, thereby maintaining data integrity and consistency across concurrent executions.

4.1   Understanding   Synchronization Primitives

In concurrent programming, the challenge of managing access to shared resources across multiple threads or goroutines necessitates specialized mechanisms. These mechanisms, known as synchronization primitives, are pivotal for ensuring data integrity and system stability. This section elaborates on the fundamental concepts underlying these primitives and their significance in developing concurrent applications.

At the core of synchronization primitives are two key objectives: mutual exclusion and coordination. Mutual exclusion is a property that ensures that only one thread or goroutine can access a critical section at any given time, thus preventing concurrent modifications that could lead to data races or inconsistent states. Coordination, on the other hand, involves managing the sequence in which threads or goroutines execute, especially in scenarios where specific operations need to occur in a particular order.

The Go programming language, recognizing the imperative of synchronization in concurrent applications, offers a comprehensive suite of primitives designed to address these objectives effectively. Among these, Mutexes and Condition Variables (Cond) stand out for their utility and widespread application.

The sync.Mutex type in Go implements a mutual exclusion lock. A mutex is essentially a token that grants its holder exclusive access to a resource. When a goroutine acquires a mutex, it gains the right to enter the critical section of code that manipulates the shared resource. Any other goroutine attempting to acquire the same mutex is blocked until the current holder releases it. This mechanism is illustrated in the following example:

```
1   var mu sync.Mutex
2
3   func criticalSection() {
4       mu.Lock()
5       // Critical section: Only one goroutine can execute this at a time.
6       mu.Unlock()
7   }
```

Another pivotal synchronization primitive is the Condition Variable, implemented in Go as sync.Cond. A Condition Variable provides a way for one or more goroutines to wait for a specific condition to become true. Unlike a mutex, which only controls access to a resource, a Condition Variable allows goroutines to suspend execution and relinquish the processor until the condition they are waiting for is signaled. The use of Condition Variables often entails a pattern where a goroutine checks a condition and, if not satisfied, waits on a Condition Variable until another goroutine modifies the state and signals the Condition Variable. A basic usage pattern for sync.Cond is as follows:

```
1  var c = sync.NewCond(&sync.Mutex{})
2  var condition bool
3
4  func waitForCondition() {
5      c.L.Lock()
6      for !condition {
7          c.Wait()
8      }
9      // Proceed with the condition satisfied.
10     c.L.Unlock()
11 }
12
13 func signalCondition() {
14     c.L.Lock()
15     condition = true
16     c.Signal() // Wake one goroutine waiting on c.
17     c.L.Unlock()
18 }
```

These examples underscore the role of synchronization primitives in facilitating safe and coordinated access to shared resources. By ensuring mutual exclusion through Mutexes and enabling goroutines to wait for or signal specific conditions via Condition Variables, Go provides developers with powerful tools for managing concurrency. These primitives are not only foundational to writing correct concurrent code but also play a critical role in optimizing performance and resource utilization in multithreaded applications.

4.2 Introduction to Mutexes

In concurrent programming in Go, the concept of mutual exclusion is paramount for safeguarding against the concurrent access of shared resources by multiple goroutines. This is where Mutexes, or mutual exclusion locks, enter the picture as one of the cornerstone mechanisms provided by Go's synchronization package, sync. A Mutex is fundamentally designed to ensure that only one goroutine can access a particular section of code or data at any given time, thereby preventing race conditions and ensuring data integrity.

The Mutex in Go's sync package is used by declaring a variable of type sync.Mutex. This Mutex has two primary methods: Lock() and Unlock(). The Lock() method is called before the code section that accesses shared resources, signaling that the current goroutine claims exclusive access to this resource. Correspondingly, the Unlock() method is invoked once the goroutine has finished its operations on the shared resources, indicating that other goroutines can now access the resource.

Here is a basic example of using a Mutex to synchronize access to a shared resource:

```
package main

import (
    "fmt"
    "sync"
)

var count int
var mutex sync.Mutex

func increment() {
    mutex.Lock()
    count++
    mutex.Unlock()
}

func main() {
    var wg sync.WaitGroup
    for i := 0; i < 100; i++ {
        wg.Add(1)
```

```
21        go func() {
22            increment()
23            wg.Done()
24        }()
25    }
26    wg.Wait()
27    fmt.Println("Count:", count)
28 }
```

In this example, a global count variable is accessed by 100 different goroutines, each attempting to increment its value by 1. The use of mutex.Lock() and mutex.Unlock() around the increment operation ensures that only one goroutine can update count at any given time. This prevents race conditions and ensures that the final value of count is indeed 100, as expected.

The output of running this program will be:

```
Count: 100
```

A crucial aspect to understand about Mutexes is their blocking nature. When a goroutine attempts to acquire a Mutex lock via the Lock() method, it will be blocked if another goroutine currently holds the lock. Only when the lock is released via Unlock() will the waiting goroutine be able to proceed. This blocking behavior is essential for coordination but also necessitates careful design to avoid deadlocks, where two or more goroutines are waiting indefinitely for each other to release locks.

To summarize, Mutexes are a fundamental tool in the Go developer's concurrency toolkit, enabling safe access to shared resources among goroutines. Proper usage of Mutexes requires a good understanding of their behavior and implications, including their blocking nature and potential for causing deadlocks if not used judiciously.

4.3   Basic Usage of a Mutex

A Mutex, or mutual exclusion lock, is a foundational tool in Go's synchronization toolkit, designed to enforce limits on access to a resource in concurrent programs. It provides a straightforward approach to ensure that only one goroutine is able to access a critical section of code at a time, effectively preventing race conditions. This section elucidates the core principles behind the basic usage of a Mutex in Go, accompanied by illustrative examples.

Firstly, a Mutex is declared by importing the sync package which provides the necessary structures for synchronization including Mutex. A Mutex must be locked (Lock()) before the critical section and unlocked (Unlock()) right after the critical section is executed. Here's a practical example demonstrating this concept:

```
 1  package main
 2
 3  import (
 4      "fmt"
 5      "sync"
 6  )
 7
 8  var (
 9      // A shared variable among goroutines
10      counter = 0
11      // Mutex to safeguard access to 'counter'
12      lock sync.Mutex
13  )
14
15  func increment() {
16      // Lock the Mutex before accessing 'counter'
17      lock.Lock()
18      // Critical section starts
19      counter++
20      // Critical section ends
21      // Unlock the Mutex after accessing 'counter'
22      lock.Unlock()
23  }
24
25  func main() {
26      const numGoroutines = 100
27      var wg sync.WaitGroup
28      wg.Add(numGoroutines)
29
30      // Create 'numGoroutines' goroutines
31      for i := 0; i < numGoroutines; i++ {
32          go func() {
33              increment()
34              wg.Done()
35          }()
36      }
37
38      wg.Wait()
39      // Expected output: 100, assuming no data race
40      fmt.Println("Counter:", counter)
```

```
41  }
```

The example above illustrates a typical usage pattern of a Mutex where a shared resource, `counter` in this case, is being accessed by multiple goroutines. The application of `lock.Lock()` and `lock.Unlock()` ensures that access to `counter` is serialized among the goroutines, hence guaranteeing that the operation of incrementing the counter is atomic. This atomicity is essential for maintaining the integrity and consistency of the data.

Upon executing the above code, the expected outcome in the console should be:

```
Counter: 100
```

This output confirms that the `counter` has been safely incremented to 100 by 100 separate goroutines without any race condition occurring. It's worth mentioning that had the Mutex not been used, the final value of `counter` could be less than 100 due to concurrent write operations leading to data races.

In practice, adhering to a few guidelines can enhance safety and readability when working with Mutexes:

- Always unlock a Mutex with a defer statement immediately after locking it, unless the unlocking needs to happen before the function returns.

- Keep the critical section as short as possible to minimize lock contention.

- Avoid recursive locks since Go's Mutex does not support re-entrancy, which can lead to deadlocks.

- Use read/write Mutex (RWMutex) when appropriate, for performance gains in scenarios with high read and low write operations.

The basic usage of a Mutex as demonstrated forms a foundation upon which more complex synchronization patterns can be built. It is a powerful primitive that, when used judiciously, can significantly enhance the robustness and safety of concurrent Go programs.

4.4   Unlocking the Power of RWMutex

The discussion now progresses to the `sync.RWMutex`, an enhancement over the simple mutex, designed to efficiently handle scenarios where the data structure is read more frequently than it is updated or written. `RWMutex` stands for Read/Write Mutex, offering separate locks for reading and writing operations. This distinction allows multiple goroutines to access the data for reading simultaneously, thus improving performance in read-heavy use cases, while still ensuring that write operations happen safely, one at a time.

To begin with, let's define the key operations of `RWMutex`:

- `Lock()` - Acquires the write lock, blocking until the lock is available if it is already held. This ensures exclusive access for writing.

- `Unlock()` - Releases the write lock. It must be called only after the lock has been successfully acquired by a call to `Lock()`.

- `RLock()` - Acquires the read lock. Multiple goroutines can hold this lock simultaneously, as long as the write lock is not held.

- `RUnlock()` - Releases the read lock. It must be called only after the lock has been successfully acquired by a call to `RLock()`.

To demonstrate the effective use of `RWMutex`, consider the following example where a shared data structure is accessed by multiple readers and a writer.

```
1  package main
2
3  import (
4      "fmt"
5      "sync"
```

```
 6      "time"
 7  )
 8
 9  type Counter struct {
10      sync.RWMutex
11      Value int
12  }
13
14  func (c *Counter) Increment() {
15      c.Lock()
16      c.Value++
17      c.Unlock()
18  }
19
20  func (c *Counter) Read() int {
21      c.RLock()
22      defer c.RUnlock()
23      return c.Value
24  }
25
26  func main() {
27      var wg sync.WaitGroup
28      counter := Counter{}
29
30      // One writer
31      wg.Add(1)
32      go func() {
33          defer wg.Done()
34          for i := 0; i < 5; i++ {
35              counter.Increment()
36              time.Sleep(1 * time.Second)
37          }
38      }()
39
40      // Multiple readers
41      for i := 0; i < 3; i++ {
42          wg.Add(1)
43          go func(id int) {
44              defer wg.Done()
45              fmt.Printf("Reader %d: %d\n", id, counter.Read())
46              time.Sleep(2 * time.Second)
47          }(i)
48      }
49
50      wg.Wait()
51  }
```

In this example, the Counter struct embeds a RWMutex. The Increment method, intended for write operations, uses Lock() and Unlock() to ensure exclusive access. In contrast, the Read method, designed for read operations, uses RLock() and RUnlock(), allowing multiple goroutines to call Read() concurrently.

When executed, the output reveals that readers are able to access the value simultaneously without waiting for other readers to complete, significantly improving throughput in read-intensive scenarios. However, writes are still serialized to maintain data integrity.

RWMutex proves invaluable in scenarios where data is read more often than written, as it allows higher concurrency for read operations. Correct usage of RWMutex can substantially enhance the performance of Go applications, particularly those dealing with large, shared data structures. Developers should assess their application's access patterns to determine whether RWMutex would provide a performance benefit over the simpler Mutex.

4.5   Deadlock: Identification and Prevention

Deadlocks are a common issue in concurrent programming, where two or more processes are unable to proceed because each is waiting for the other to release a resource. In Go, deadlocks can occur when goroutines hold a mutex while waiting for another, leading to a situation where none of the goroutines can continue. This section will address the mechanisms to identify and prevent deadlocks, particularly focusing on the use of mutexes.

Identifying Deadlocks

To identify a deadlock, it is crucial to understand the conditions that lead to this state. A deadlock can occur if and only if all of the following four conditions are met simultaneously:

- **Mutual Exclusion**: A resource can be held by only one process at a time.

- **Hold and Wait**: A process holding at least one resource is waiting to acquire additional resources held by other processes.

- **No Preemption**: A resource can be released only voluntarily by the process holding it, after that process has completed its task.

- **Circular Wait**: A set of processes are waiting for each other in a circular form, where each process is waiting for a resource held by the next process in the chain.

Understanding these conditions helps in diagnosing deadlocks in a concurrent Go application. Tools such as the Go runtime's deadlock detector can also aid in identifying deadlocks during development by automatically detecting situations where goroutines are stuck waiting indefinitely.

Preventing Deadlocks

Prevention of deadlocks entails altering the way resources are managed so that at least one of the deadlock conditions is not met. Here are several techniques used in Go to prevent deadlocks:

- **Lock Ordering**: Establish and enforce a global order in which locks are acquired. If all goroutines acquire locks in a consistent order, the circular wait condition cannot hold, thus preventing deadlocks.

- **Lock Timeout**: Use try-lock patterns or timeouts when attempting to acquire a mutex. This strategy prevents a process from waiting indefinitely for a resource, thus addressing the hold and wait condition.

```
1   type Account struct {
2       balance int
3       mutex sync.Mutex
4   }
5
6   func Transfer(a, b *Account, amount int) {
7       timeout := time.After(1 * time.Second)
8       for {
9           a.mutex.Lock()
10          if b.mutex.TryLock() {
11              // Perform the transfer
12              a.balance -= amount
13              b.balance += amount
14              b.mutex.Unlock()
15              a.mutex.Unlock()
16              return
17          } else {
```

```
18        a.mutex.Unlock()
19        select {
20        case <-timeout:
21            fmt.Println("Transfer timed out")
22            return
23        default:
24            // Retry the transfer
25        }
26      }
27    }
28  }
```

- **Avoid Holding Multiple Locks**: Whenever possible, design your concurrency structure such that a goroutine does not need to hold more than one mutex at a time. This can usually be achieved by designing higher-level abstractions that encapsulate the complexity of multiple resources.

- **Use of Higher-Level Primitives**: Consider using higher-level synchronization primitives provided by Go, like channels, which have built-in mechanisms to avoid common deadlock scenarios.

While deadlocks can be challenging to identify and prevent, understanding their causes and employing strategies to mitigate the conditions leading to deadlocks can substantially reduce their occurrence. Properly designing synchronization around mutexes, employing lock ordering, utilizing timeouts, and leveraging Go's higher-level primitives are effective ways to ensure that your applications remain responsive and deadlock-free.

4.6   Introduction to Condition Variables

Condition variables are a crucial synchronization primitive in concurrent programming that work in tandem with mutex locks to enable goroutines to wait for certain conditions to be true before proceeding. In Go, this is facilitated through the sync.Cond type, which is built on top of a mutex or RWMutex. This section elucidates the concept of condition variables, their role in synchronization, and how they assimilate within the Go ecosystem to provide a powerful mechanism for controlling access and flow in concurrent operations.

A condition variable essentially allows one or more goroutines to wait for a specific condition to become true. While it is technically possible to achieve a similar effect by repeatedly checking the condition in a busy loop, this approach is inefficient as it consumes CPU cycles and can lead to processor contention. Condition variables, in contrast, are a more sophisticated and efficient way to handle such synchronization needs.

To effectively leverage sync.Cond in Go, it is vital to understand the following three key methods:

- NewCond: This function initializes a new condition variable. It requires a sync.Locker as an argument, which typically is a sync.Mutex or sync.RWMutex. The locker serves to safeguard access to the shared resource or condition.

- Wait: This method suspends the execution of the calling goroutine until the condition it is waiting upon changes. Before calling Wait, the goroutine must acquire the lock on the mutex associated with the condition variable. Wait automatically releases the lock and re-acquires it once the condition has changed and the goroutine is ready to proceed.

- Signal and Broadcast: These methods are used to wake up goroutines that are waiting on the condition variable. Signal wakes up one waiting goroutine, while Broadcast wakes up all waiting goroutines. After awakening, the goroutines compete to acquire the lock on the mutex.

An important aspect of using condition variables effectively is understanding the relationship between the condition being awaited, the condition variable itself, and the mutex used to lock the condition. All three components work together to ensure that access to the shared resource is synchronized and that goroutines wait or proceed based on an accurate understanding of the current state of the system.

Consider the following example demonstrating the use of a condition variable in a producer-consumer scenario:

```go
package main

import (
    "fmt"
    "sync"
    "time"
)

var (
    cond = sync.NewCond(&sync.Mutex{})
    queue []int
)

func producer() {
    for {
        cond.L.Lock()
        if len(queue) == 10 {
            cond.L.Unlock()
            time.Sleep(time.Millisecond * 100)
            continue
        }
        item := produceItem()
        queue = append(queue, item)
        fmt.Printf("Produced: %d\n", item)
        cond.Signal()
        cond.L.Unlock()
        time.Sleep(time.Millisecond * 100)
    }
}

func consumer() {
    for {
        cond.L.Lock()
        for len(queue) == 0 {
            cond.Wait()
        }
        item := queue[0]
        queue = queue[1:]
        fmt.Printf("Consumed: %d\n", item)
        cond.L.Unlock()
        time.Sleep(time.Millisecond * 100)
    }
}

func main() {
    go producer()
    go consumer()
    select {}
}

func produceItem() int {
    return rand.Intn(100)
}
```

In this example, a producer goroutine produces items and adds them to a queue. If the queue reaches a certain size, in this case, 10, the producer stops producing until there is more room. Correspondingly, a consumer goroutine consumes items from the queue. The condition variable, 'cond', is used to signal the consumer when a new item is produced and to make the producer wait when the queue is full.

Condition variables, succinctly, offer a means to coordinate the operations of multiple goroutines based on the state of shared resources, making them invaluable for developing concurrent applications in Go where precise synchronization is requisite for maintaining data integrity and performance.

4.7 Using Cond for Synchronization

The preceding sections explored the fundamentals of mutexes and their critical role in protecting shared resources in concurrent Go applications. Moving forward, we pivot our focus to another significant synchronization primitive provided by Go's sync package: the Condition Variable, commonly referred to as Cond. A Cond is typically used in scenarios where one or more goroutines wait for a certain condition to become true before proceeding. This is particularly useful in managing complex synchronization tasks, such as coordinating the sequence of operations across different goroutines.

To instantiate a Cond, one must first have a sync.Locker, usually a sync.Mutex or sync.RWMutex, which serves as the underlying locker for the condition variable. The creation of a Cond variable can be achieved as follows:

```
var mutex sync.Mutex
cond := sync.NewCond(&mutex)
```

Once a Cond has been established, the primary methods of interest are Wait(), Signal(), and Broadcast(). The Wait() method is invoked by a goroutine to suspend its execution until the condition it awaits is signaled. Before calling Wait(), the goroutine must acquire the locker (e.g., mutex) associated with the Cond. Upon calling Wait(), the goroutine atomically unlocks the mutex and suspends execution. When the condition is eventually signaled, the goroutine awakens, re-acquires the mutex, and proceeds.

To demonstrate the use of Cond for synchronization, consider a simplified example where multiple worker goroutines wait for a "start signal" from the main goroutine before commencing execution:

```
1   var (
2       mutex sync.Mutex
3       ready bool
4       cond = sync.NewCond(&mutex)
5   )
6
7   func worker(id int) {
8       mutex.Lock()
9       for !ready {
10          cond.Wait()
11      }
12      mutex.Unlock()
13      fmt.Printf("Worker %d starts\n", id)
14  }
15
16  func main() {
17      for i := 0; i < 3; i++ {
18          go worker(i)
19      }
20
21      // Ensure all workers are ready to start.
22      time.Sleep(time.Second)
23      mutex.Lock()
24      ready = true
25      mutex.Unlock()
26      cond.Broadcast()
27
28      // Wait for all workers to complete.
29      time.Sleep(time.Second)
30  }
```

In this example, multiple worker goroutines are initiated. Each worker immediately locks the mutex and checks a shared variable ready. Since ready is initially false, the workers call cond.Wait(), which atomically unlocks the mutex and suspends the goroutine. When the main goroutine sets ready to true, it calls cond.Broadcast(), which wakes up all waiting goroutines. The workers then re-acquire the mutex, confirm ready is now true, and proceed with their execution.

Signaling a condition is done using either `Signal()` or `Broadcast()`. `Signal()` wakes one waiting goroutine, typically used when the condition becomes true for at least one waiter. Conversely, `Broadcast()` awakens all waiting goroutines, applicable when the condition becomes true for all waiters. The choice between `Signal()` and `Broadcast()` depends on the specific synchronization logic required by the application.

This section has elucidated the use of `Cond` for synchronization, emphasizing its utility in scenarios necessitating the coordination of goroutine execution based on the satisfaction of specific conditions. `Cond` facilitates complex synchronization logic that goes beyond the binary locking mechanism offered by mutexes, thereby enabling more refined control over goroutine coordination and execution sequence. In the following sections, we will explore building higher-level synchronization primitives leveraging the capabilities of `Cond` and other synchronization tools provided by Go.

4.8 Building Higher Level Synchronization Primitives

This section demonstrates the process of constructing high-level synchronization primitives using Mutexes and Cond. These advanced constructs are necessary when the existing primitives do not suffice for nuanced synchronization needs in more complex Go applications.

Custom Barrier Implementation

A barrier is a synchronization construct that allows multiple goroutines to wait at a certain point until all have reached this point, after which they can all proceed. In Go, this can be achieved by combining Mutex and Cond.

To begin, define a structure `Barrier` which holds a count of goroutines to wait for, a total count as a goal, a mutex, and a condition variable:

```
1  type Barrier struct {
2      mtx sync.Mutex
3      cond *sync.Cond
4      count int
5      total int
6  }
```

Next, implement a constructor function for creating an instance of Barrier:

```
1  func NewBarrier(total int) *Barrier {
2      b := &Barrier{
3          total: total,
4          count: 0,
5      }
6      b.cond = sync.NewCond(&b.mtx)
7      return b
8  }
```

The core function of the Barrier is Wait, which will block the calling goroutine until the count matches the total number set for the barrier:

```
1  func (b *Barrier) Wait() {
2      b.mtx.Lock()
3      b.count++
4      if b.count < b.total {
5          b.cond.Wait()
6      } else {
7          b.cond.Broadcast()
8          b.count = 0 // Reset for potential reuse
9      }
10     b.mtx.Unlock()
11 }
```

The Wait function increments the count and checks if it is less than the total. If so, it waits for a broadcast. Once the count equals the total, a broadcast signal is sent, allowing all waiting goroutines to proceed. The count is reset for potential reuse.

Semaphore Implementation

A semaphore controls access to a common resource by multiple goroutines in the concurrency environment, where the number of goroutines accessing the resource is limited to a specified maximum.

To build a semaphore, we introduce a struct `Semaphore`:

```
type Semaphore struct {
    mtx sync.Mutex
    cond *sync.Cond
    max int
    cur int
}
```

Constructor for Semaphore:

```
func NewSemaphore(max int) *Semaphore {
    s := &Semaphore{
        max: max,
        cur: 0,
    }
    s.cond = sync.NewCond(&s.mtx)
    return s
}
```

The `Semaphore` has two primary methods, `Acquire` and `Release`, managing access to the controlled resource:

```
func (s *Semaphore) Acquire() {
    s.mtx.Lock()
    for s.cur == s.max {
        s.cond.Wait()
    }
    s.cur++
    s.mtx.Unlock()
}

func (s *Semaphore) Release() {
    s.mtx.Lock()
    s.cur--
    s.cond.Signal()
    s.mtx.Unlock()
}
```

The `Acquire` method locks the semaphore and waits until the current count is less than the maximum allowed. It then increments the current count and releases the lock. The `Release` method decrements the current count and signals a waiting goroutine that it might now proceed.

By utilizing Mutexes and Cond, we crafted high-level synchronization mechanisms, the Barrier, and Semaphore, which provide more granular control over goroutine coordination. These constructs enhance the capability to tackle more sophisticated synchronization challenges within concurrent Go applications, thereby broadening the scope of problems that can be efficiently solved with Go's concurrency model.

4.9   Best Practices for Mutexes and Cond

In concurrent programming with Go, correctly utilizing synchronization primitives like Mutexes and Condition Variables (Cond) is paramount for ensuring data integrity and preventing race conditions. This section will delineate best practices to adhere to when employing these primitives to enhance the efficacy and robustness of Go applications.

Adherence to Minimal Locking Principle

The minimal locking principle advocates for holding locks for the shortest time possible. This practice mitigates the risk of creating bottlenecks, thereby enhancing application performance. The following guidelines help adhere to this principle:

- Limit the scope of critical sections by only protecting the code segment that accesses shared resources.

- Avoid long-running computations or I/O operations within locked sections.

- Use defer statements to ensure mutexes are unlocked as soon as the critical section ends.

Deadlock Prevention

Deadlocks occur when two or more goroutines wait on each other to release locks, leading to a standstill. Best practices for prevention include:

- Employ a consistent locking order across the application.

- Utilize a timeout for lock acquisition attempts.

- Leverage the 'TryLock' functionality, if available, to avoid blocking.

Effective Use of RWLock

The sync.RWMutex type should be used when a resource is read more often than written to. This type allows multiple readers to hold the lock concurrently, but only one writer. This practice enhances concurrency by allowing multiple reads to occur in parallel. It is critical, however, to ensure that writes are still adequately protected and serialized.

Proper Use of Condition Variables

Condition Variables should be used judiciously for signaling and waiting for specific conditions rather than general locking purposes. The following practices should be observed:

- Always recheck the condition in a loop after waiting, since spurious wakeups can occur.

```
1  cond.L.Lock()
2  for !condition() {
3      cond.Wait()
4  }
5  // Proceed with logic
6  cond.L.Unlock()
```

- Use broadcast sparingly, as waking up all waiting goroutines might lead to a thundering herd problem. Prefer signal if only one goroutine needs to wake up.

Avoidance of Locking for Signals Only

For cases where the sole purpose is to signal goroutines without protecting shared data, using channels is recommended over mutex and

117

condition variables. Channels in Go offer a more intuitive and less error-prone means for synchronization in such scenarios.

Regular Profiling and Monitoring

To ensure that these best practices yield the desired effect, it's indispensable to perform regular profiling and monitoring of the application. Go's toolchain provides powerful profiling tools that can identify bottlenecks and help developers understand where synchronization might be inefficient or unnecessary.

Documentation and Code Review

Finally, meticulous documentation of the locking strategy and conducting thorough code reviews can significantly alleviate the complexities involved in concurrent programming. Peer reviews help identify potential misuse of synchronization primitives and ensure adherence to established best practices.

Employing Mutexes and Condition Variables effectively demands a deep understanding of their behavior and implications on application performance and concurrency. Following the outlined best practices can significantly mitigate common pitfalls and enhance the robustness and efficiency of Go applications.

4.10   Comparison Between Channels and Mutexes for Synchronization

In Go, both mutexes and channels serve as powerful tools for handling synchronization in concurrent programming. However, they are designed with different philosophies and use cases in mind. This section meticulously dissects the operational characteristics, benefits, and limitations of each, providing a comparative perspective to guide the choice between them for specific synchronization needs.

Philosophical Underpinnings and Primary Use Cases

Mutexes: At their core, mutexes are about protecting shared state. They ensure that only one goroutine can access a piece of data at a time, which is critical for preventing data races. Mutexes are relatively low-level primitives and are typically used in scenarios where fine-grained control over data access is required.

Channels: Channels, on the other hand, embody the philosophy of "communicating sequential processes" (CSP). They are not just about protecting data but also about coordinating the execution flow among goroutines. Channels enable goroutines to synchronize without sharing memory, primarily through sending and receiving messages. This makes channels a higher-level construct compared to mutexes, ideal for tasks that involve complex synchronization patterns or communication among goroutines.

Performance Considerations

When it comes to performance, the choice between mutexes and channels depends on the specific use case:

- Use of mutexes is generally faster for simply protecting data access, as they incur less overhead than channels.

- Channels can introduce more latency due to the message-passing overhead, especially in high-contention scenarios.

However, optimizing for performance without considering the design's clarity and maintainability can lead to suboptimal code. It's essential to balance performance with code simplicity and readability.

Readability and Code Structure

- **Mutexes** require explicit locking and unlocking operations, which can clutter the code and introduce the risk of deadlocks if not handled correctly.

- **Channels**, being a higher-level construct, often lead to cleaner and more readable code. They encourage a style of coding where synchronization and communication are explicitly modeled as message passing, reducing the risk of subtle bugs.

Nevertheless, channels can also complicate code if used excessively or inappropriately, especially when simpler mutex-based synchronization would suffice.

Best Practices and Recommendations

Deciding between using mutexes or channels hinges on understanding the specific requirements and constraints of the synchronization problem:

- For protecting shared variables or implementing simple state synchronization, mutexes are often the most straightforward and efficient choice.

- For coordinating complex concurrent workflows or when goroutine communication is needed, channels offer a more expressive and potentially safer abstraction.

In practice, combining both mutexes and channels in the same application is not uncommon. For example, using mutexes for protecting shared state while using channels for signaling and coordinating between goroutines can leverage the strengths of both primitives.

Both mutexes and channels are indispensable tools in the concurrent programming toolkit provided by Go. The choice between them should be informed by their distinct characteristics and the specific needs of the application. By understanding the comparative strengths and weaknesses outlined above, developers can make informed decisions, leading to more robust, efficient, and maintainable Go applications.

4.11   Real-world Scenarios: When to Use Mutexes vs. Channels

In the Go programming environment, effectively managing concurrent execution is pivotal for creating efficient and reliable applications. This section elucidates the practical applications of Mutexes and Channels, guiding developers on when to leverage each to synchronize access to shared resources or coordinate the execution flow among goroutines.

Mutex for Managing Shared State

Mutexes are quintessential for scenarios where shared state modification necessitates exclusive access to ensure data integrity. Consider a web service that maintains a global count of requests processed. This counter is incremented each time a request is handled, necessitating synchronization to prevent race conditions.

```
import (
    "sync"
)

var (
    counter int64
    counterMu sync.Mutex
)

func incrementCounter() {
    counterMu.Lock()
    counter++
    counterMu.Unlock()
}
```

In this example, `counterMu.Lock()` and `counterMu.Unlock()` encapsulate the critical section, ensuring that the `counter` variable is incremented atomically by one goroutine at a time, thereby safeguarding the counter's integrity.

Channels for Communicating Among Goroutines

Channels shine in scenarios where direct communication among goroutines is essential. A common use case is the implementation of the Producer-Consumer pattern, where one or more producers generate items for consumption, and one or more consumers process those items.

```
 1  package main
 2
 3  import "fmt"
 4
 5  func producer(ch chan<- int) {
 6      for i := 0; i < 10; i++ {
 7          ch <- i
 8      }
 9      close(ch)
10  }
11
12  func consumer(ch <-chan int) {
13      for item := range ch {
14          fmt.Println("Consumed", item)
15      }
16  }
17
18  func main() {
19      ch := make(chan int)
20      go producer(ch)
21      consumer(ch)
22  }
```

This code snippet demonstrates a basic Producer-Consumer setup. The producer function sends integers to the consumer through the ch channel, which in turn processes these integers. Channels here provide a clean, lock-free mechanism for data exchange between goroutines, preventing the complexities associated with lock management.

Deciding Between Mutexes and Channels

Deciding whether to use Mutexes or Channels primarily depends on the nature of the problem at hand. As a general guideline:

- Use Mutexes when you need to protect shared state that is accessed by multiple goroutines. They are particularly useful when the operation on the shared state is brief and the state itself is not naturally represented as a sequence of values.

- Use Channels when the problem can be structured around the communication of data values or events. They are especially adept at solving coordination problems without explicitly managing lock state, making the code more readable and maintainable.

In some advanced scenarios, a hybrid approach combining both Mutexes and Channels might be the best solution. This approach can leverage the strengths of both synchronization primitives to achieve more complex synchronization tasks that would be less efficient or more difficult to implement using either one in isolation.

To encapsulate, understanding the specific requirements of your concurrent programming task is paramount in choosing the correct synchronization primitive. While Mutexes are tailored for exclusive access to shared state, Channels excel in orchestrating goroutines and data flow. Adeptly using them in tandem or in isolation can significantly enhance the efficiency and reliability of Go applications.

4.12 Advanced Techniques with Mutexes and Cond

When working with concurrent processes, the intricacy of inter-thread communication and resource sharing necessitates advanced synchronization mechanisms beyond simple lock acquisition and release. This section will delve into sophisticated patterns and practices for employing Mutexes and Condition Variables (Cond) in Go, aiming to enhance the efficiency and reliability of concurrent applications.

Optimizing Mutex Performance

Mutexes, while crucial for ensuring data consistency, can significantly impact performance when not used judiciously. Two advanced techniques, read-write locks and lock-free structures, can mitigate these performance drawbacks.

Leveraging RWMutex for Read-heavy Workloads

The sync package in Go offers RWMutex, a specialized mutex that distinguishes between read and write locks, allowing multiple readers to access the resource concurrently, provided no write operation is taking place. This is particularly beneficial for scenarios where data is read frequently but modified less often.

```
1   var cache = make(map[string]string)
2   var rwMutex sync.RWMutex
3
4   func Read(key string) string {
5       rwMutex.RLock()
6       value := cache[key]
7       rwMutex.RUnlock()
8       return value
9   }
10
11  func Write(key, value string) {
12      rwMutex.Lock()
13      cache[key] = value
14      rwMutex.Unlock()
15  }
```

In the above example, multiple calls to Read can execute simultaneously without blocking each other, promoting higher throughput in read-heavy use cases.

Lock-free Data Structures

Another advanced strategy involves using atomic operations and lock-free data structures to avoid locking entirely. While this approach can drastically increase performance, it requires a deep understanding of memory ordering and is generally more complex to implement correctly.

```
1   var value atomic.Value
2
3   func Update(newValue string) {
4       value.Store(newValue)
5   }
6
7   func Read() string {
8       return value.Load().(string)
9   }
```

Here, `atomic.Value` provides a safe way to modify and access a shared value without explicit locks.

Efficient Use of Condition Variables

Condition Variables (Cond) in Go facilitate waiting for or announcing the occurrence of specific conditions. Efficient use involves minimizing unnecessary wakes and ensuring that conditions are correctly rechecked after a wake-up.

Signaling vs. Broadcasting

Cond provides two methods for waking waiting goroutines: `Signal` and `Broadcast`. `Signal` wakes one arbitrary goroutine, while `Broadcast` wakes all waiting goroutines. Using `Signal` is more efficient when only one goroutine can make progress, whereas `Broadcast` is appropriate when a change potentially allows multiple goroutines to proceed.

```
1    var cond = sync.NewCond(&sync.Mutex{})
2    var ready bool
3
4    func worker() {
5        cond.L.Lock()
6        for !ready {
7            cond.Wait()
8        }
9        // perform work
10       cond.L.Unlock()
11   }
12
13   func main() {
14       go worker()
15       // prepare work
```

```
16    cond.L.Lock()
17    ready = true
18    cond.Signal() // or cond.Broadcast() if multiple workers are waiting
19    cond.L.Unlock()
20 }
```

Avoiding Spurious Wakes and Deadlocks

When using Cond, it's crucial to recheck the condition upon wakeup, as wakes might be spurious, and the anticipated condition may not yet be true.

```
1  cond.L.Lock()
2  for !condition() {
3      cond.Wait()
4  }
5  // Proceed with the assumption that the condition is true
6  cond.L.Unlock()
```

This pattern ensures that the goroutine only proceeds when the condition it's waiting for is indeed satisfied, safeguarding against both spurious wakes and potential deadlocks.

Understanding and applying these advanced techniques with Mutexes and Cond variables can significantly enhance the performance and reliability of concurrent Go applications. By judiciously employing read-write locks, exploring lock-free data structures, and making efficient use of condition variables, developers can optimize synchronization mechanisms to achieve high-performing, correct concurrent applications.

Chapter 5

Advanced Channel Patterns

Building on the foundational understanding of channels, this chapter delves into advanced patterns that exploit channels' full potential in Go's concurrent programming model. It covers sophisticated techniques such as pipeline construction, fan-in and fan-out operations, and patterns for combining, distributing, or throttling tasks among goroutines. By exploring these advanced channel patterns, readers will learn how to structure more complex concurrent operations efficiently, enabling the development of highly scalable and performant Go applications that effectively manage communication and synchronization among goroutines.

5.1   Revisiting Channel Basics

Channels are a fundamental concept in Go's concurrency model, allowing goroutines to communicate safely without explicit locks or condition variables. This section aims to solidify the understanding of channels, emphasizing their behavior, types, and operations.

Understanding Channels in Go

At its core, a channel is a communication pipe that connects concurrent goroutines in a Go program. Channels ensure that data exchanges between goroutines are synchronized, hence preventing race conditions and ensuring data integrity. To declare a channel in Go, the chan keyword is used, followed by the type of data the channel will transport.

```
var messageChan chan string
```

This code snippet declares a channel named messageChan, which is designed to carry strings. However, before using this channel, it must be initialized. Channel initialization is achieved using the make function.

```
messageChan = make(chan string)
```

Sending and Receiving from Channels

Channels support two primary operations: sending and receiving data. The arrow operator (<-) is utilized to denote the direction of data flow.

Sending to a Channel: To send data to a channel, place the channel variable on the left side of the arrow operator, and the data to be sent on the right.

```
messageChan <- "Hello, Channels!"
```

Receiving from a Channel: Conversely, to receive data from a channel, the arrow operator points towards the variable intended to hold the received data.

```
receivedMessage := <-messageChan
```

Closing Channels

Closing a channel signifies that no more data will be sent on that channel. This operation is critical for preventing goroutine leaks and for channels involved in range loops.

```
close(messageChan)
```

128

After a channel is closed, it is still possible to receive data from the channel, provided there is data queued in the channel. However, sending data to a closed channel results in a runtime panic.

Buffered versus Unbuffered Channels

Channels in Go can be either buffered or unbuffered, determined at the time of initialization by the buffer capacity argument passed to the make function.

- *Unbuffered Channels*: These channels have no buffer, meaning send operations block until another goroutine is ready to receive the data.

```
1  unbufferedChan := make(chan int)
```

- *Buffered Channels*: These channels have a finite buffer, allowing send operations to proceed without blocking if the buffer is not full.

```
1  bufferedChan := make(chan int, 10)
```

It's crucial to select the appropriate channel type based on the specific requirements and behavior of the goroutines in your Go program.

Select Statements

The select statement provides another level of sophistication in managing multiple channel operations. It allows a goroutine to wait on multiple communication operations, proceeding with the first one that becomes available.

```
1  select {
2  case msg := <-chan1:
3      fmt.Println("Received from chan1:", msg)
4  case chan2 <- "Hello":
5      fmt.Println("Sent to chan2")
6  default:
7      fmt.Println("No communication")
8  }
```

The default case in a select statement is optional and runs if no other case is ready.

129

Mastering the basics of channel operations and understanding the distinction between buffered and unbuffered channels are pivotal in leveraging Go's powerful concurrency model effectively. These concepts form the foundation upon which more complex concurrent patterns and operations can be built, as explored in subsequent sections of this chapter.

5.2   Buffered Channels Deep Dive

Buffered channels in Go extend the basic capabilities of unbuffered channels by allowing channels to store multiple values before blocking. This capability introduces additional complexity and power in managing concurrent operations, making understanding their behavior essential.

Let's start with the creation of buffered channels. To instantiate a buffered channel, the make function is used, specifying the channel's type and its capacity:

```
1   ch := make(chan int, 5)
```

This line of code creates a buffered channel ch capable of holding up to 5 integers. Unlike unbuffered channels, which block senders until the message is received, buffered channels block senders only when the channel is full. Similarly, receivers block only when the channel is empty.

The fundamental operations on buffered channels – sending, receiving, and closing – resemble those on unbuffered channels. However, the semantics around blocking behavior differ due to the buffer. For sending operations, if the channel's buffer is full, the goroutine blocks until space becomes available. Conversely, if the buffer is not full, the send operation succeeds immediately, without blocking:

```
1   ch <- 42
```

Receiving from a buffered channel checks if there are any items in the channel's buffer. If the buffer is not empty, the receive operation retrieves an item from the buffer and proceeds without blocking. If the buffer is empty, the receiver blocks until an item is sent to the channel:

```
1  value := <-ch
```

Closing a buffered channel is similar to closing an unbuffered channel. It signals that no more values will be sent on the channel. Receivers can still receive any remaining items in the buffer until it gets emptied:

```
1  close(ch)
```

A critical aspect of working with buffered channels is managing the buffer's capacity efficiently. Overfilling a buffer can lead to blocked goroutines, while underutilizing a buffer may result in unnecessary synchronization overhead. Therefore, choosing the right size for the channel's buffer is crucial for achieving desired performance characteristics.

Buffered channels can be used to implement various concurrent patterns, such as worker pools. In such patterns, a buffered channel acts as a job queue, with multiple producer goroutines sending jobs to the channel and worker goroutines receiving jobs from it. The buffer size controls the maximum number of jobs that can be queued, providing a mechanism for limiting concurrency:

```
1  jobs := make(chan Job, 100)
```

This sets up a buffered channel capable of holding up to 100 jobs. Producer goroutines may send jobs to this channel, and worker goroutines may concurrently receive and process jobs from it.

In summary, understanding and leveraging the characteristics of buffered channels is pivotal in crafting efficient and responsive concurrent Go programs. Through careful consideration of buffer sizes and the concurrency patterns in your application, buffered channels can be a powerful tool in your concurrent programming arsenal.

5.3   Pattern: Pipeline

The concept of a pipeline in the context of concurrent programming in Go utilizes channels to chain together a series of processing steps— each represented by goroutines—where the output of one step is the input for the next. This pattern enables efficient data processing and transformation through a sequence of operations.

To illustrate the pipeline pattern, consider a scenario where we need to process a series of integers. The processing involves three stages: multiplication, addition, and filtering. Each of these stages will be encapsulated in its goroutine and connected via channels.

The first step involves defining the input to the pipeline. This usually takes the form of a generator function, which takes a variadic slice of integers as input and returns a channel through which these integers are sent.

```go
func generate(numbers ...int) <-chan int {
    out := make(chan int)
    go func() {
        for _, n := range numbers {
            out <- n
        }
        close(out)
    }()
    return out
}
```

The next step in constructing our pipeline is the multiplication stage. This stage reads integers from the input channel, multiplies each by a predefined factor, and sends the result to the output channel.

```go
func multiply(input <-chan int, factor int) <-chan int {
    out := make(chan int)
    go func() {
        for n := range input {
            out <- n * factor
        }
        close(out)
    }()
    return out
}
```

Following multiplication, the addition stage receives each multiplied integer, adds a constant value to it, and forwards the sum to the next channel.

```go
func add(input <-chan int, additive int) <-chan int {
    out := make(chan int)
    go func() {
        for n := range input {
            out <- n + additive
        }
        close(out)
    }()
    return out
}
```

Lastly, a filter stage can be implemented to only allow numbers fulfilling a certain condition to pass through. For instance, filtering out even numbers:

```go
func filterEven(input <-chan int) <-chan int {
    out := make(chan int)
    go func() {
        for n := range input {
            if n%2 == 0 {
                out <- n
            }
        }
        close(out)
    }()
    return out
}
```

To wire up these stages into a pipeline, channels from one stage are connected to the subsequent stage as inputs.

```go
numbers := generate(1, 2, 3, 4)
multiplied := multiply(numbers, 2)
added := add(multiplied, 1)
filtered := filterEven(added)

for n := range filtered {
    fmt.Println(n)
}
```

The output of running this program would be the processed integers that made it through each stage of the pipeline:

```
4
6
8
```

The pipeline pattern in Go effectively encapsulates the concept of a series of transformations or computations, allowing for parallel execution and efficient data processing. By decomposing complex processes into discrete stages connected by channels, developers can implement sophisticated data processing pipelines that are both clear in intent and efficient in execution.

5.4   Pattern: Fan-in and Fan-out Revisited

Fan-out and fan-in patterns represent two pivotal methodologies in enhancing the efficiency and responsiveness of concurrent Go programs. By revisiting these patterns, we aim to deepen the understanding and application of these constructs, demonstrating their crucial roles in building scalable and robust applications.

Understanding Fan-out

Fan-out is a concurrency pattern utilized to distribute tasks among multiple goroutines to parallelize work. In a typical fan-out scenario, a single goroutine sends work tasks to multiple worker goroutines through a channel. Each worker goroutine operates on the tasks concurrently, thus speeding up the overall execution time.

Consider the following implementation example:

```
func fanOut(tasks []Task, numWorkers int) {
    taskCh := make(chan Task)

    for i := 0; i < numWorkers; i++ {
        go func() {
            for task := range taskCh {
                process(task)
            }
        }()
    }

    for _, task := range tasks {
        taskCh <- task
    }
    close(taskCh)
}
```

In this example, tasks is a slice of Task objects to be processed, and numWorkers represents the number of goroutines to distribute these tasks across. The call to process(task) represents the work done on each task by a worker goroutine.

Understanding Fan-in

Conversely, the fan-in pattern is employed to combine results from multiple worker goroutines into a single channel. This pattern is particularly useful for consolidating results or performing operations that require aggregating data from multiple concurrent sources.

Here is an implementation example of the fan-in pattern:

```
func fanIn(channels ...<-chan Result) <-chan Result {
    var wg sync.WaitGroup
    merged := make(chan Result)

    output := func(c <-chan Result) {
        for result := range c {
            merged <- result
        }
        wg.Done()
    }

    wg.Add(len(channels))
    for _, c := range channels {
        go output(c)
    }

    go func() {
        wg.Wait()
        close(merged)
    }()

    return merged
}
```

In the above code, channels is a variadic parameter that accepts an arbitrary number of read-only channels of Result objects. The function launches a goroutine for each input channel that forwards all received results to a single merged channel. After all input channels are drained and closed, the merged channel is then closed to signal completion.

Combining Fan-out and Fan-in

The real power emerges when combining fan-out and fan-in patterns together. By distributing work across multiple worker goroutines (fan-out) and aggregating their results (fan-in), concurrent applications can achieve significant performance improvements and maintain cleaner code architectures.

Consider this high-level example:

```
func processTasksConcurrently(tasks []Task, numWorkers int) <-chan Result {
    // Fan-out: Distribute tasks to worker goroutines
    taskCh := make(chan Task)
    for i := 0; i < numWorkers; i++ {
        go worker(taskCh)
    }
    go func() {
        for _, task := range tasks {
            taskCh <- task
        }
        close(taskCh)
    }()

    // Collect individual worker channels into a slice
    workerChs := make([]<-chan Result, numWorkers)
    for i := range workerChs {
        workerChs[i] = worker(taskCh)
    }

    // Fan-in: Merge the results from all workers
    return fanIn(workerChs...)
}
```

By incorporating both fan-out and fan-in patterns, the processTasksConcurrently function illustrates a powerful approach to distribute a slice of tasks among a defined number of workers and then consolidate their outcomes efficiently. This method is especially beneficial in scenarios requiring concurrent processing of tasks followed by an aggregation or synthesis of their results.

In summary, by mastering the fan-out and fan-in patterns and understanding when and how to apply them together, developers can significantly enhance the performance and scalability of concurrent Go applications.

5.5   Pattern: Or-done Channel

Or-done channels are a design pattern that enhances the flow control in Go's concurrent systems, making it easier to handle situations where one wishes to proceed only if an operation is completed or a certain condition is met. This pattern is particularly useful in managing multiple goroutines where the completion of at least one goroutine is required to progress. It encapsulates the complexity of monitoring multiple channel operations, allowing the developer to focus on the business logic rather than the intricacies of concurrency primitives.

The essence of this pattern lies in its ability to amalgamate the completion signals from multiple channels into a single channel. This unified channel then conveys the message that at least one of the monitored operations is done, signaling the system to move forward. The implementation involves the creation of a special 'or-done' function, which takes in an arbitrary number of channels as its input and returns a single channel. The returned channel closes as soon as any input channel closes, indicating that the operation linked with that channel is completed.

Implementing the Or-done Channel Pattern

Let's start with implementing the 'or-done' function. The function will utilize Go's 'select' statement to listen to multiple channels simultaneously. As soon as one of these channels closes, the function will close the return channel as well.

```
1   func orDone(done <-chan interface{}, c <-chan interface{}) <-chan
        interface{} {
2     valStream := make(chan interface{})
3     go func() {
4       defer close(valStream)
5       for {
6         select {
7         case <-done:
8           return
9         case val, ok := <-c:
10          if !ok {
```

137

```
11                    return
12                }
13                select {
14                case valStream <- val:
15                case <-done:
16                }
17            }
18        }
19    }()
20    return valStream
21 }
```

In this implementation, 'done' is a channel that signals the cancellation of the operation, and 'c' is the input channel from which the data is received. The function returns a channel ('valStream'), which is immediately returned and populated in a separate goroutine. The 'select' statement inside the goroutine listens for two possible events: the closure of the 'done' channel, which signals immediate termination, and the reception of a value from channel 'c'. If a value is received from 'c', it is sent to 'valStream' unless the 'done' channel is closed, signaling that no further values should be sent.

Using the Or-done Channel Pattern

To illustrate the usage of the or-done channel pattern, consider a scenario where there are multiple data streams, and the goal is to process data from any channel as soon as it becomes available. Using the 'orDone' function simplifies the implementation by abstracting the complexity of handling multiple channels.

```
1  // Assume stream1 and stream2 are channels from which data is received
2  stream1 := make(chan interface{})
3  stream2 := make(chan interface{})
4
5  // Simulated goroutines to send data on the channels
6  go func() {
7      defer close(stream1)
8      // Simulate data sending
9  }()
10
11 go func() {
12     defer close(stream2)
```

```
13      // Simulate data sending
14   }()
15
16   done := make(chan interface{})
17   defer close(done)
18
19   for val := range orDone(done, stream1) {
20      // Process val
21   }
22
23   for val := range orDone(done, stream2) {
24      // Process val
25   }
```

This example demonstrates how to apply the or-done channel pattern to manage data streams. By wrapping the input channels with 'orDone', the program can gracefully handle completion signals from multiple sources, thereby enhancing the readability and maintainability of concurrent Go code.

The or-done channel pattern exemplifies the power of Go's concurrency model, facilitating elegant solutions to complex synchronization problems. By understanding and applying this pattern, developers can write concise and robust concurrent programs that are both efficient and easy to reason about.

5.6   Pattern: Tee Channel

The Tee Channel pattern stands out in concurrent programming by not only facilitating the distribution of a stream of data across different components but also by allowing simultaneous consumption of the same data stream. This section will dissect the intricacies of the Tee Channel pattern, focusing primarily on its implementation and utility within the Go programming environment.

The essence of the Tee Channel pattern lies in its ability to split a single input channel into two identical output channels. Data read from the input channel is replicated and forwarded to both output channels, thereby allowing two distinct goroutines to process the same stream of data concurrently. This pattern is particularly useful in sce-

139

narios where the same data needs to be processed in different manners or when ensuring redundant processing for fault tolerance.

Implementing the Tee Channel pattern involves creating a function that accepts an input channel and returns two output channels. Consider the following implementation:

```
1  func tee(done <-chan struct{}, in <-chan interface{}) (_, _ <-chan interface{})
      {
2     out1 := make(chan interface{})
3     out2 := make(chan interface{})
4     go func() {
5         defer close(out1)
6         defer close(out2)
7         for val := range in {
8             var out1, out2 = out1, out2
9             for i := 0; i < 2; i++ {
10                select {
11                case <-done:
12                    return
13                case out1 <- val:
14                    out1 = nil
15                case out2 <- val:
16                    out2 = nil
17                }
18            }
19        }
20    }()
21    return out1, out2
22  }
```

This function accepts a done channel and an input channel in as arguments. It returns two output channels, out1 and out2. Inside the function, a goroutine is spawned to read from the input channel and write each value to both output channels. The use of the done channel enables cancellation of the operation, ensuring that the function respects graceful shutdown semantics.

One notable application of the Tee Channel pattern is in data monitoring systems, where the same data stream is analyzed for different metrics. For example, one output channel might be connected to a component that calculates the average value, while the other channel forwards the data to a component checking for outliers or anomalies.

The Tee Channel pattern, however, introduces some challenges. Proper error handling and synchronization become crucial, as there are now multiple receivers from a single data source. Care must be taken to ensure that all receivers are ready to consume the data to prevent data loss or deadlock situations. Additionally, the pattern can introduce a bottleneck if one of the downstream consumers processes data significantly slower than the other, potentially leading to unbounded memory consumption if the incoming data rate is high.

The Tee Channel pattern is a powerful tool in the Go concurrency model, enabling parallel consumption of data streams. It allows for flexible and efficient data processing architectures but requires careful consideration of error handling, synchronization, and resource management to ensure robust and performant implementations.

5.7 Pattern: Bridge Channel

The Bridge Channel pattern in Go's concurrent programming is designed to dynamically merge several channels into a single channel. This pattern is particularly useful when there is a need to consume values from an arbitrary number of channels in a situation where the exact number of channels is unknown at compile time, or it changes dynamically at runtime. By implementing the Bridge Channel pattern, developers can simplify the process of reading from multiple input channels simultaneously, thereby enhancing the flexibility and scalability of their concurrent applications.

To understand how to implement the Bridge Channel pattern, let's consider a scenario where there is a need to consolidate values from multiple channels into one. This is achieved by creating a function that takes a slice of channels as its input and returns a single channel as its output. The returned channel is where the merged output from all input channels will be sent.

The implementation involves two key steps:

- Launching a goroutine for each input channel, which reads values from the input and sends them to an intermediary channel.

- Merging outputs from intermediary channels into a single output channel.

Here is an example to demonstrate this:

```
1   package main
2
3   import (
4       "fmt"
5       "sync"
6   )
7
8   // bridge takes a slice of channels and returns a single channel that
9   // closes when all input channels are closed and all values have been sent.
10  func bridge(done <-chan struct{}, chanStream <-chan (<-chan int)) <-chan int {
11      valStream := make(chan int)
12      go func() {
13          var wg sync.WaitGroup
14          for {
15              var stream <-chan int
16              select {
17              case maybeStream, ok := <-chanStream:
18                  if !ok {
19                      // If chanStream is closed, start termination process
20                      go func() {
21                          wg.Wait()
22                          close(valStream)
23                      }()
24                      return
25                  }
26                  stream = maybeStream
27              case <-done:
28                  return
29              }
30              wg.Add(1)
31              go func() {
32                  for val := range stream {
33                      select {
34                      case valStream <- val:
35                      case <-done:
36                          return
37                      }
38                  }
39                  wg.Done()
40              }()
41          }
42      }()
43      return valStream
44  }
45
46  // Example usage
47  func main() {
48      done := make(chan struct{})
49      defer close(done)
50
51      // Simulate a situation where we have three channels
52      chan1 := make(chan int)
```

```
53      chan2 := make(chan int)
54      chan3 := make(chan int)
55
56      chanStream := make(chan (<-chan int), 3)
57      chanStream <- chan1
58      chanStream <- chan2
59      chanStream <- chan3
60
61      go func() {
62          defer close(chanStream)
63          defer close(chan1)
64          defer close(chan2)
65          defer close(chan3)
66
67          // Simulating sending data to the channels
68          for i := 0; i < 10; i++ {
69              chan1 <- i
70              chan2 <- i + 10
71              chan3 <- i + 20
72          }
73      }()
74
75      // Create a bridge channel that combines all channels into one
76      for v := range bridge(done, chanStream) {
77          fmt.Println(v)
78      }
79  }
```

In this example, the bridge function takes two parameters: a done channel for cancellation and a chanStream, which is a channel of channels broadcasting int values. Each read from the chanStream produces a new channel from which the bridge should start reading and sending values to an output channel, valStream. As each input channel closes, the bridge function continues reading values from remaining channels. Once all input channels are exhausted and closed, the output channel valStream is also closed, signaling that the bridging process is complete.

The Bridge Channel pattern thus enables the consolidation of multiple data streams into a single stream, facilitating easier and more effective management of dynamic data flows in concurrent Go applications.

5.8   Cancellable Goroutines and Channels

In concurrent programming, controlling the lifecycle of goroutines
is an essential aspect of managing resource utilization and ensuring
that your Go applications behave predictably, especially in dynamic
conditions where tasks may need to be prematurely terminated. This
section focuses on strategies for implementing cancellable goroutines
and channels, which can significantly enhance the robustness and
flexibility of your program.

Goroutines, in their simplest form, execute independently; they can
be thought of as lightweight threads. However, unlike threads that
may have built-in mechanisms to be interrupted or terminated, goroutines must be explicitly managed to support cancellation. A common approach to achieving this involves the use of a pattern that utilizes cancellation channels.

Using Cancellation Channels

The idea behind this pattern is straightforward: a dedicated
channel, referred to as a cancellation channel, is used to signal a
goroutine to terminate its execution.   The goroutine checks for
signals on this channel at appropriate points in its execution flow to
determine whether it should continue running or terminate.

```
 1  func cancellableGoroutine(done chan bool) {
 2      for {
 3          select {
 4          case <-done:
 5              return // Terminate the goroutine
 6          default:
 7              // Perform regular operation
 8          }
 9      }
10  }
```

In the above code snippet, the function `cancellableGoroutine` takes
a channel done as an argument. Inside the function, a `select` statement is used to listen for a signal on the done channel. If a signal is
received, the goroutine returns, hence terminating its execution. Otherwise, it proceeds with its regular operations.

To initiate the cancellation of the goroutine, you simply close the done channel from another goroutine or the main function. Since a close operation on a channel is broadcasted to all receivers, the signal is effectively propagated, ensuring that any listening goroutines can respond accordingly.

```
1  done := make(chan bool)
2  go cancellableGoroutine(done)
3  // At some point later, when cancellation is desired
4  close(done)
```

Context Package for Cancellation

While the cancellation channel pattern is effective, the Go standard library offers a more sophisticated way to manage cancellations through the context package. The context package enables not only cancellation signals but also carrying request-scoped values, deadlines, and timeouts across API boundaries and between processes.

To create a context with cancellation capabilities, you use the context.WithCancel function. This function returns a copy of the parent context and a cancel function. Calling the cancel function cancels the context, which can be detected by calling the Done method on the context.

```
1   ctx, cancel := context.WithCancel(context.Background())
2   go func() {
3       select {
4       case <-ctx.Done():
5           return // Terminate on cancellation.
6       default:
7           // Regular operation
8       }
9   }()
10
11  // When cancellation is needed
12  cancel()
```

Using the context package for cancellations provides a standardized, powerful way to manage goroutine lifecycles, especially in complex applications with multiple concurrent operations that may require precise control over goroutine termination.

The ability to cancel goroutines and manage their execution flow is crucial for building reliable concurrent applications in Go. Whether using cancellation channels directly or leveraging the context package, Go provides the necessary constructs to effectively manage goroutine lifecycles. Understanding and applying these patterns will significantly contribute to the stability and performance of your Go applications.

5.9   Timeouts and Heartbeats

Timely feedback is crucial in concurrent systems to ensure they perform optimally and detect potential failures early. This section discusses two patterns that provide such feedback within the Go concurrency model: timeouts and heartbeats.

Timeouts

Timeouts prevent a Go application from waiting indefinitely for an operation to complete. This is particularly useful when working with operations that may stall due to issues like network latency or deadlock situations. Implementing timeouts in Go can be achieved through the use of the time.After function, which returns a channel that sends the current time after a specified duration.

Consider a scenario where a goroutine needs to receive data from a channel but should not wait longer than 2 seconds. This can be implemented as follows:

```
select {
case res := <-dataChannel:
    // Process the received data
    fmt.Println("Received data:", res)
case <-time.After(2 * time.Second):
    fmt.Println("Operation timed out")
}
```

In this example, if no data is received on dataChannel within 2 seconds, the time.After channel sends a signal, and the timeout case gets executed.

Heartbeats

Heartbeats are a mechanism to periodically signal operational status from a goroutine. They are useful in monitoring the health of concurrent operations and ensuring the system is active. Implementing a heartbeat involves sending a pulse on a dedicated channel at regular intervals.

The following example demonstrates how a heartbeat can be integrated into a long-running operation:

```
1   heartbeat := make(chan struct{})
2   go func() {
3       for {
4           select {
5           case <-time.After(1 * time.Second):
6               // Send a heartbeat pulse
7               heartbeat <- struct{}{}
8           // Include other case blocks for the actual operation
9           }
10      }
11  }()
12
13  // Monitor the heartbeat in a separate goroutine
14  go func() {
15      for {
16          select {
17          case <-heartbeat:
18              fmt.Println("Pulse")
19          case <-time.After(5 * time.Second):
20              fmt.Println("Operation seems stalled")
21              return
22          }
23      }
24  }()
```

In this setup, the operation goroutine sends a pulse every second. Meanwhile, another goroutine monitors these pulses. If it does not receive a pulse within 5 seconds, it logs a message indicating the operation may have stalled.

These patterns, timeouts and heartbeats, when appropriately utilized, can greatly enhance the reliability and maintainability of concurrent Go applications. They allow developers to enforce operation constraints and monitor the health state of goroutines, which are essential practices for building robust concurrent systems.

5.10   Error Propagation in Channel-based Systems

Error handling is a crucial component in robust concurrent Go applications. Channels in Go, through their communication mechanisms, offer a unique advantage in error propagation among concurrent goroutines. This section discusses strategies for effectively propagating errors in channel-based systems, ensuring that errors do not go unnoticed and are handled gracefully.

The Need for Error Channels

Typically, functions return an error value alongside their expected result, allowing the caller to handle any errors that arise. In concurrent operations, where functions may be executed in goroutines, direct return values are not feasible. Instead, channels serve as the conduit for both data and errors. This necessitates the creation of dedicated error channels, alongside data channels, to facilitate error propagation.

```
1   // Create a dedicated error channel
2   errChan := make(chan error)
```

Sending Errors through Channels

When an error occurs within a goroutine, it should be sent through the error channel to be handled by the receiver. This approach ensures that the error is not lost in the asynchronous operation.

```
1   go func() {
2       err := performTask()
3       if err != nil {
4           errChan <- err
5           return
6       }
7   }()
```

Receiving Errors

On the receiving end, one must listen to the error channel alongside the data channel. This can be done effectively using a `select` statement, which allows the receiver to react to whichever channel receives a message first.

```
select {
case err := <-errChan:
    // Handle error
case data := <-dataChan:
    // Handle data
}
```

Pattern: Wrapping Errors with Context

To enhance error handling, wrapping errors with additional context before sending them through the channel can provide receivers with more information, aiding in debugging and error recovery strategies.

```
go func() {
    err := performTask()
    if err != nil {
        wrappedErr := fmt.Errorf("task failed: %w", err)
        errChan <- wrappedErr
        return
    }
}()
```

Best Practices for Error Channels

- Always initialize error channels where there's a possibility of goroutines failing.

- Consider buffering error channels if multiple goroutines might encounter errors simultaneously, to prevent goroutines from blocking on send operations.

- Use `select` with a default case when sending errors to non-buffered channels, to avoid blocking if the receiver is not ready to handle the error.

- Ensure error channels are closed appropriately when all operations are complete to prevent memory leaks.

Handling Multiple Errors

In systems where multiple errors can occur, aggregating these errors into a single error representation can simplify error handling for the receiver. This can be achieved by listening to the error channel in a dedicated goroutine, collecting errors as they occur, and acting on them collectively after all operations have concluded.

```
errors := make([]error, 0)
go func() {
    for err := range errChan {
        errors = append(errors, err)
    }
    // Handle collected errors
}()
```

By adopting these strategies for error propagation in channel-based systems, Go developers can ensure that errors are effectively communicated and handled, contributing to more reliable and robust concurrent applications.

5.11   Dynamic Channel Composition

Dynamic channel composition in Go allows for the construction and management of channel operations at runtime, offering a versatile approach to handling multiple channels simultaneously. This capability harnesses the full potential of Go's concurrency model, especially in scenarios where the number of channels and goroutines interacting with them can vary dynamically.

The foundation of dynamic channel composition lies in the `select` statement, which provides a powerful mechanism to wait on multiple channel operations. By combining `select` with reflection, specifically the `reflect.Select` function, it is possible to construct a dynamically adaptable select block.

The first step in implementing dynamic channel composition is understanding the signature and functionality of `reflect.Select`. This function requires a slice of `reflect.SelectCase` structures, each representing a channel operation (send or receive) to be considered in the selection process. The `reflect.Select` function returns the index of the case that executed along with the received value, if applicable, and a boolean indicating whether the channel was closed.

Consider the following example where we dynamically select from a slice of channels:

```
1   package main
2
3   import (
4       "fmt"
5       "reflect"
6       "time"
7   )
8
9   func main() {
10      ch1 := make(chan int)
11      ch2 := make(chan int)
12
13      go func() {
14          time.Sleep(1 * time.Second)
15          ch1 <- 10
16      }()
17
18      go func() {
19          time.Sleep(2 * time.Second)
20          ch2 <- 20
21      }()
22
23      var cases []reflect.SelectCase
24      cases = append(cases, reflect.SelectCase{Dir: reflect.SelectRecv, Chan:
            reflect.ValueOf(ch1)})
25      cases = append(cases, reflect.SelectCase{Dir: reflect.SelectRecv, Chan:
            reflect.ValueOf(ch2)})
26
27      chosen, value, ok := reflect.Select(cases)
28
29      if ok {
30          fmt.Printf("Read from channel %d: %d\n", chosen+1, value.Int())
31      } else {
32          fmt.Println("Channel was closed")
33      }
34  }
```

In this example, two goroutines send values to `ch1` and `ch2` after different durations. The main goroutine creates a slice of `reflect.SelectCase`, each representing a receive operation on these channels. The `reflect.Select` call then dynamically selects whichever channel is ready to receive first, prints the value, and terminates.

Dynamic channel composition is particularly useful in situations where the set of channels to select from is not known at compile time or varies dynamically during the program execution. This pattern enables developers to write more flexible and adaptable concurrent code by abstracting over the channels being selected.

However, it is essential to use this technique judanisusly, as reflection incurs a performance cost compared to static `select` statements. The use of reflection should be justified by the need for dynamic behavior that cannot be easily achieved with static code constructs.

In summary, dynamic channel composition with `reflect.Select` provides a powerful tool for complex concurrent scenarios in Go, allowing programs to interact with an arbitrary number of channels in a scalable and efficient manner.

5.12   Building Custom Synchronization Constructs

While Go's standard library provides a rich set of primitives for managing concurrency, such as goroutines and channels, there are scenarios where the provided constructs may not perfectly align with the specific synchronization requirements of a given problem. In these cases, developers have the option to build custom synchronization constructs that better suit their needs. This section explores methods and practices for creating such constructs, focusing on leveraging Go's existing concurrency primitives to build more specialized synchronization mechanisms.

Firstly, it is essential to understand the importance of minimizing shared state and the role of immutability in reducing complexity and potential for synchronization issues. Keeping these principles in mind can guide the design of your custom constructs towards being more robust and easier to reason about.

Using Channels to Build Synchronization Primitives

Channels in Go are versatile tools not only for data exchange between goroutines but also as synchronization primitives. Let's explore how to utilize channels to create custom synchronization constructs, such as a barrier that allows goroutines to wait for each other before proceeding.

Barrier Pattern

A barrier is a common synchronization pattern where a group of goroutines must wait at a certain point in the code until all goroutines have reached this point. Implementing a barrier can be achieved by combining channels and a counter to track the number of goroutines waiting.

```
func NewBarrier(n int) (*Barrier, chan bool) {
    barrier := make(chan bool)
    count := 0
    mu := sync.Mutex{}

    return func() {
        mu.Lock()
        count++
        if count == n {
            close(barrier)
        }
        mu.Unlock()

        <-barrier
    }, barrier
}
```

In this example, NewBarrier function returns a closure that goroutines can call to wait at the barrier and a channel that is closed when all goroutines have reached the barrier. The mutex mu is used to protect the access to the shared count variable.

153

Combining Channels and Select Statements for Complex Synchronization

The select statement in Go is a powerful feature for managing multiple channel operations. It can be used creatively to combine channels for building advanced synchronization patterns, such as a multiplexer that combines multiple input channels into a single output channel, preserving the order of messages.

Multiplexer Pattern

The multiplexer pattern involves combining multiple input channels into a single output channel, ensuring that messages from the input channels are forwarded to the output channel in the order they are received.

```
1   func Multiplex(inputs ...<-chan int) <-chan int {
2       var wg sync.WaitGroup
3       output := make(chan int)
4
5       send := func(c <-chan int) {
6           for n := range c {
7               output <- n
8           }
9           wg.Done()
10      }
11
12      wg.Add(len(inputs))
13      for _, c := range inputs {
14          go send(c)
15      }
16
17      go func() {
18          wg.Wait()
19          close(output)
20      }()
21
22      return output
23  }
```

This multiplexer function takes a variable number of input channels and returns a single output channel. It starts a goroutine for each input channel that forwards messages to the output channel. The WaitGroup is used to track when all input channels have been drained and it is safe to close the output channel.

Designing and implementing custom synchronization constructs requires a deep understanding of Go's concurrency patterns and primitives. By creatively combining channels, select statements, mutexes, and other synchronization mechanisms provided by the Go runtime, developers can build efficient and robust custom constructs tailored to their specific requirements. This not only enhances the capability to manage complex synchronization scenarios but also contributes to writing more maintainable and scalable Go applications.

Chapter 6

Select Statement: Multiplexing with Channels

The select statement in Go is a powerful control structure that allows a program to wait on multiple channel operations, effectively enabling multiplexing. This mechanism is pivotal in writing concurrent programs that can elegantly handle different kinds of communications, such as simultaneous sends or receives on multiple channels. This chapter provides an in-depth exploration of the select statement, illustrating its syntax, use cases, and combining it with other concurrency primitives to develop robust Go applications. Through mastering the select statement, developers gain the ability to implement sophisticated concurrent patterns, enhance responsiveness, and improve the overall structure of their Go programs.

6.1   Introduction to the Select Statement

The select statement in Go is a distinctive control structure that empowers concurrent programming by facilitating the wait on multiple channel operations. It stands as a cornerstone for developers looking to implement multiplexing within their applications, an essential technique for managing simultaneous communication streams. This unique feature of Go not only enhances the language's capability in handling concurrency but also simplifies the complexity involved in such operations.

Understanding the select statement begins with recognizing its role in concurrent programming. At its core, the select statement allows a goroutine to wait on multiple communication operations, including channel send and receive operations. The main advantage here is the ability to block a goroutine until one of its cases can proceed, which is pivotal in ensuring that programs do not waste resources by polling or exhibit unnecessary latency.

The syntax of the select statement is straightforward yet powerful, permitting developers to elegantly express complex concurrent logic. A typical select statement is structured as follows:

```
1  select {
2  case <-chan1:
3      // Execute logic when a message is received from chan1
4  case chan2 <- value:
5      // Execute logic when able to send a value to chan2
6  default:
7      // Execute if no other case is ready (optional)
8  }
```

Each case within a select block is associated with a channel operation, and the select statement blocks until one of its cases can proceed. This mechanism enables developers to write highly responsive applications that can handle multiple communication events concurrently, without resorting to complex and error-prone synchronization techniques.

An essential feature of the select statement is its ability to work seamlessly with the default case. This case is executed if no other case is ready, making it possible to implement non-blocking

158

channel operations. Such functionality is particularly useful in scenarios where the program needs to remain responsive, even if the expected communications have not occurred.

Furthermore, the `select` statement's compatibility with the `for` loop opens avenues for building sophisticated patterns of communication. By combining these two constructs, developers can construct robust event loops that continuously monitor and react to channel activities. This pattern is incredibly effective in server-side applications, where managing multiple client connections and data streams is a common requirement.

In summary, the `select` statement is an indispensable tool in the Go programmer's toolkit, unlocking the full potential of concurrent programming. Its ability to wait on multiple channel operations simultaneously simplifies the construction of complex communication structures, thus paving the way for writing efficient, responsive, and maintainable concurrent applications.

6.2   Syntax and Basic Use Cases

The `select` statement in Go is a unique and crucial feature for managing multiple channel operations. It allows a goroutine to wait on several communication operations simultaneously. Understanding its syntax is fundamental to leveraging its full potential in concurrent programming.

The basic syntax of a `select` statement is as follows:

```
1   select {
2   case <-chan1:
3       // Do something when data is received from chan1
4   case chan2 <- data:
5       // Do something when data can be sent to chan2
6   default:
7       // Optional: Do something if no other case is ready
8   }
```

In the above structure, each `case` statement specifies a channel operation, either send or receive. The `select` statement blocks until one of its cases can proceed, at which point it executes that case. If multiple cases could proceed, one is chosen at random to execute.

The default case is optional and is executed if none of the channel operations are immediately ready. This allows for implementing non-blocking channel operations.

Basic Use Cases

Let's explore some basic use cases of the select statement to understand its practical applications.

- **Sending or Receiving on a Single Channel:** If there is only one channel involved, the select statement can be used to attempt send or receive operations without blocking indefinitely.

```
1  select {
2  case msg := <-messages:
3      fmt.Println("Received", msg)
4  case <-time.After(1 * time.Second):
5      fmt.Println("No message received in 1 second")
6  }
```

- **Simultaneously Waiting on Multiple Channels:** The primary use case of select is when a goroutine needs to wait on multiple channels at the same time, responding as soon as any one of them has data available.

```
1  select {
2  case msg1 := <-chan1:
3      fmt.Println("Received from chan1:", msg1)
4  case msg2 := <-chan2:
5      fmt.Println("Received from chan2:", msg2)
6  }
```

- **Implementing Timeout:** The select statement is particularly useful for implementing timeouts to prevent goroutines from blocking indefinitely on channel operations.

```
1  select {
2  case res := <-c:
3      fmt.Println(res)
4  case <-time.After(3 * time.Second):
5      fmt.Println("Operation timed out")
6  }
```

- **Non-blocking Channel Operations:** By including a `default` case, `select` statements can be used to perform non-blocking sends or receives.

```
1  select {
2  case msg := <-ch:
3      fmt.Println("Received", msg)
4  default:
5      fmt.Println("No message")
6  }
```

These basic use cases illustrate the flexibility and power of the `select` statement in Go. By effectively utilizing `select`, developers can write more robust and responsive concurrent applications.

6.3   Select with Multiple Channels

The power of the select statement in Go programming is profoundly realized when it is employed to operate on multiple channels concurrently. This capability underlines the essence of concurrent programming in Go, enabling the development of highly efficient and responsive applications that can handle various forms of communication simultaneously. This section elucidates the mechanism of using select with multiple channels, outlining its syntax, providing concrete examples, and discussing practical use cases to enlighten the reader on how to leverage this feature in real-world applications.

To comprehend the usage of select with multiple channels, it is essential to first grasp its basic syntax:

```
1  select {
2  case msg1 := <-chan1:
3      // Handle the message received from chan1
4  case msg2 := <-chan2:
5      // Handle the message received from chan2
6  default:
7      // Execute if no message is received from any channel
8  }
```

The syntax above illustrates a select statement waiting on two channel operations. The 'case' clauses represent the operations to perform based on which channel receives a message first. If neither

161

chan1 nor chan2 has a message ready, the 'default' case is executed, ensuring the select statement does not block indefinitely unless it is the desired behavior.

The following example showcases a more practical application, demonstrating how to concurrently process input from multiple channels using the select statement:

```
package main

import (
    "fmt"
    "time"
)

func main() {
    chan1 := make(chan string)
    chan2 := make(chan string)

    go func() {
        time.Sleep(1 * time.Second)
        chan1 <- "Message from channel 1"
    }()

    go func() {
        time.Sleep(2 * time.Second)
        chan2 <- "Message from channel 2"
    }()

    for i := 0; i < 2; i++ {
        select {
        case msg1 := <-chan1:
            fmt.Println("Received:", msg1)
        case msg2 := <-chan2:
            fmt.Println("Received:", msg2)
        }
    }
}
```

This program creates two channels, chan1 and chan2, and starts two goroutines that each send a message through one of the channels after a delay. The select statement in the main function waits for messages from these channels, handling whichever message arrives first. By iterating the select statement twice, the program ensures that it receives and processes the message from both channels before terminating.

In practice, the select statement's capacity to listen to multiple channels simultaneously is invaluable for a myriad of applications, such as:

- Implementing multiplexing to improve data handling efficiency in network servers.

- Merging inputs from multiple sources to be processed in a single pipeline.

- Facilitating non-blocking channel operations by including a default case.

Furthermore, when employing the select statement with multiple channels, developers need to be aware of potential pitfalls, such as deadlocks and race conditions. Correct structuring of channel operations and careful program design are paramount to mitigate these issues.

Lastly, the agility and concurrency control offered by the select statement with multiple channels are integral to achieving high performance in Go applications. Mastering its usage is thus essential for developers looking to unlock the full potential of concurrent programming in Go.

6.4 Default Case: Non-blocking Operations

In this section, we will discuss the inclusion of a default case in a select statement to facilitate non-blocking operations. The default case in Go's select statement allows the program to execute an alternative action if no other case is ready. This pattern is crucial for preventing a Go routine from becoming indefinitely blocked, enhancing the responsiveness and efficiency of concurrent applications.

A select statement without a default case blocks until one of its cases can proceed. Conversely, including a default case ensures that the select statement always has an executable path, thus never blocking. This mechanism is particularly valuable when a program must remain responsive to new inputs or when operations need to proceed even in the absence of new data or events.

Consider the following simplified example, where a non-blocking read is implemented using a select statement with a default case:

```
1  select {
2  case msg := <-messages:
3     fmt.Println("Received message:", msg)
4  default:
5     fmt.Println("No new message received.")
6  }
```

In this example, if the messages channel has data ready to be read, the first case executes, and the message is printed. If the messages channel is empty, rather than blocking while waiting for a message, the select statement immediately falls through to the default case, printing "No new message received."

The non-blocking pattern is also useful for write operations. Here's how a non-blocking send operation could be structured:

```
1  select {
2  case messages <- msg:
3     fmt.Println("Sent message:", msg)
4  default:
5     fmt.Println("Message not sent. Channel full or no receiver.")
6  }
```

In this case, if the messages channel is ready to accept a new message (*e.g.*, it has buffer space available), the message is sent, and the first print statement executes. If the channel is not ready (because it is unbuffered and has no receiver or its buffer is full), the program executes the default case, indicating that the message was not sent.

Using the default case for non-blocking operations is a powerful tool, but it requires careful design consideration. The immediate execution of the default case may lead to busy waiting if used in a tight loop without any other form of rate limiting or sleep. To mitigate this, it is often wise to combine non-blocking operations with other concurrency mechanisms or a time.Sleep call to prevent excessive CPU usage.

To conclude, employing a default case in select statements for non-blocking operations enables more flexible and responsive concurrent Go applications. It allows a program to attempt

164

operations like sending to or receiving from a channel without getting stuck, offering alternative behavior when immediate progress is not possible. This pattern is a key part of writing efficient, non-blocking code in concurrent Go applications.

6.5   Select for Timeout Handling

Handling timeouts in concurrent programming is critical to prevent a program from hanging indefinitely while waiting for an operation that may never complete. Go provides an elegant way to handle timeouts using the select statement in combination with time.After. This technique is essential for developing responsive applications that can deal with delays or unresponsive external services gracefully.

First, let's examine the basic structure of using select for timeout handling:

```
select {
case result := <-operationChan:
    // Handle successful operation
case <-time.After(time.Second * 10):
    // Handle timeout after 10 seconds
}
```

In this example, `operationChan` is a channel where a concurrent operation sends its result. The `time.After` function creates a channel and sends the current time after the specified duration, in this case, 10 seconds. The select statement waits for either the operation to send a result or for the timeout to occur, whichever happens first. This pattern ensures that the program can proceed without waiting longer than the timeout period.

It is important to note that `time.After` is not the only way to implement timeouts but is the most straightforward for many use cases. However, when managing resources carefully or handling many timeouts in a tight loop, creating a new timer for each timeout with `time.After` can lead to excessive resource use. In such scenarios, a more efficient approach involves reusing timers.

Here's an example of reusing a timer for multiple timeouts:

```
timer := time.NewTimer(time.Second * 10)
defer timer.Stop()

select {
case result := <-operationChan:
    // Handle successful operation
case <-timer.C:
    // Handle timeout
}

// Reset the timer for another operation
if !timer.Stop() {
    <-timer.C
}
timer.Reset(time.Second * 10)
```

In this advanced usage, a timer is created once with `time.NewTimer` and can be stopped and reset as needed. This approach is particularly useful in loops or instances where multiple operations might need to be timed out sequentially or concurrently, reducing the overhead of creating and garbage collecting many timers.

The select statement's ability to handle timeouts enhances the robustness of concurrent operations by enabling developers to specify maximum allowable durations for operations that could otherwise block indefinitely. This is especially useful when interacting with external services where response times can be unpredictable. By incorporating timeout handling using select, Go programs can achieve increased responsiveness and reliability.

6.6   Dynamic Select with reflect.Select

The `select` statement in Go is inherently static, meaning it requires all channels and cases to be known at compile time. However, certain scenarios necessitate dynamic selection from an arbitrary number of channels at runtime. This is where `reflect.Select` comes into play, offering a mechanism to dynamically select over a set of channel operations.

To understand the use of `reflect.Select`, it is critical to grasp that it operates with slices of `reflect.SelectCase`. Each `SelectCase` represents a single case in a select statement, encapsulating the operation (send or receive), the channel on which the operation is performed, and the send value, if the operation is a send.

```
 1  import "reflect"
 2
 3  // Dynamically select from a slice of channels
 4  func dynamicSelect(channels []reflect.SelectCase) {
 5      chosen, value, ok := reflect.Select(channels)
 6
 7      if !ok {
 8          fmt.Println("The chosen channel was closed")
 9          return
10      }
11
12      fmt.Printf("Received from channel %d: %v\n", chosen, value)
13  }
```

This code snippet demonstrates a simple function that accepts a slice of reflect.SelectCase, performs a dynamic selection, and then prints the index of the selected case along with the value received. The third return value, ok, is a boolean indicating whether the receive operation was successful or the channel was closed.

It is important to note that constructing the slice of reflect.SelectCase requires careful attention to the kind of operation each case represents. Here's how to prepare a slice of SelectCase for both sending and receiving operations:

```
 1  // Creating a slice of reflect.SelectCase
 2  var cases []reflect.SelectCase
 3
 4  // Adding receive case
 5  cases = append(cases, reflect.SelectCase{
 6      Dir: reflect.SelectRecv,
 7      Chan: reflect.ValueOf(recvChan),
 8  })
 9
10  // Adding send case
11  cases = append(cases, reflect.SelectCase{
12      Dir: reflect.SelectSend,
13      Chan: reflect.ValueOf(sendChan),
14      Send: reflect.ValueOf(sendValue),
15  })
16
17  // Adding default case
18  cases = append(cases, reflect.SelectCase{
19      Dir: reflect.SelectDefault,
20  })
```

This example demonstrates the process of constructing a slice containing three types of `SelectCase`: one for receiving, one for sending, and a default case. Each case requires specifying the direction (`Dir`) of the operation using `reflect.SelectRecv` for receives, `reflect.SelectSend` for sends, and `reflect.SelectDefault` for the default case. The channel (`Chan`) and send value (`Send`) are specified as reflected values obtained with `reflect.ValueOf`.

The dynamic nature of `reflect.Select` makes it a powerful tool in scenarios where the number or identity of channels is not known until runtime. However, this flexibility comes with the cost of performance and readability compared to static `select` statements. Therefore, `reflect.Select` should be used judiciously, when the benefits of dynamic channel selection outweigh these drawbacks.

`reflect.Select` extends the capabilities of Go's concurrency model by enabling dynamic selection across a varying number of channels. By understanding how to correctly construct and utilize `reflect.SelectCase`, developers can incorporate this dynamic behavior into their concurrent Go applications, tackling scenarios that are not possible with the static `select` statement alone.

6.7   Select and Loop Patterns

The effective combination of select statements with loop constructs in Go can lead to powerful patterns that enhance the handling of concurrent operations. These patterns are essential for developers to understand as they offer mechanisms to control and manage multiple channels and their interactions within loops. This section will discuss the integration of select statements within for loops, detailing scenarios where such patterns are practical and how to implement them correctly.

First, let's consider a basic for loop incorporating a select statement:

```
1  for {
2      select {
3      case msg1 := <-channel1:
4          fmt.Println("Received", msg1)
```

```
5      case msg2 := <-channel2:
6          fmt.Println("Received", msg2)
7          }
8  }
```

This loop will perpetually wait for messages from either `channel1` or `channel2`, printing out the received message. The beauty of this pattern lies in its simplicity and efficiency in dealing with concurrent communications. However, developers must be cautious about the potential for infinite loops unless a break condition or a timeout is implemented.

Incorporating a timeout pattern within a select statement in a loop can manage long waits or deadlock scenarios. The following example demonstrates this:

```
1  timeout := time.After(5 * time.Second)
2  for {
3      select {
4      case msg := <-channel:
5          fmt.Println("Received", msg)
6      case <-timeout:
7          fmt.Println("Timeout, no messages received.")
8          break
9          }
10 }
```

In this example, a timeout channel is created using the `time.After` function, which will send the current time after a specified duration, in this case, 5 seconds. The select statement waits for a message from the channel or the timeout event, whichever occurs first, thus preventing the loop from running indefinitely.

Another common pattern is utilizing the default case to perform non-blocking operations within a loop. This pattern allows the loop to execute other tasks while waiting for channel operations. See the example below:

```
1  for {
2      select {
3      case msg := <-channel:
4          fmt.Println("Received", msg)
5      default:
6          fmt.Println("No message received, performing other operations.")
7          // Perform non-blocking operations here
8          }
9  }
```

Here, if no message is ready to be received from the channel, the default case is executed, allowing the loop to continue performing other tasks rather than blocking on channel operations.

Furthermore, dynamic channel selection within loops can be achieved using the `reflect.Select` function. This advanced pattern allows the select operation to include an arbitrary number of cases, determined at runtime. The implementation of this pattern requires careful construction of select case lists using reflection, which is beyond the scope of basic select and loop patterns but is an important area for advanced Go concurrency practices.

Combining select statements with loops enables developers to construct efficient and responsive concurrent programs in Go. By understanding and applying these patterns, developers can effectively manage multiple channels and concurrent operations, leading to more robust and scalable applications.

6.8   Preventing Goroutine Leaks

Goroutine leaks in Go are a subtle yet common problem that can lead to increased memory usage and eventual degradation of application performance over time. A goroutine leak occurs when a goroutine is blocked indefinitely, unable to proceed or terminate, thus remaining alive and consuming system resources. This section elucidates strategies to prevent goroutine leaks, focusing on the prudent use of the `select` statement along with other concurrency primitives.

A primary cause of goroutine leaks is blocked channel operations where a goroutine attempts to send or receive on a channel, but no corresponding receive or send operation occurs. For instance, a goroutine blocked on a channel send operation because there's no receiver for the data can lead to a leak. To mitigate this, always ensure that every send operation has a corresponding receive operation and vice versa.

The following code snippet demonstrates a potential goroutine leak scenario:

```
1  func leakyFunction() {
2      ch := make(chan int)
3      go func() {
4          val := 42
5          ch <- val // This send operation can block indefinitely
6          fmt.Println("Value sent to channel")
7      }()
8  }
```

In the example above, the goroutine may block indefinitely when trying to send val to the channel ch if there is no corresponding receive operation. This can cause a goroutine leak.

To prevent such leaks, especially in complex applications where it might not be immediately clear if a corresponding operation exists, the select statement in conjunction with a timeout can be employed. The select statement with a default case for non-blocking operations or a timeout case using time.After provides a way to escape blocking operations if they cannot proceed within a reasonable time.

```
1  func leakPreventFunction() {
2      ch := make(chan int)
3      go func() {
4          select {
5          case ch <- 42:
6              fmt.Println("Value sent to channel")
7          case <-time.After(1 * time.Second):
8              fmt.Println("Timeout: aborting send operation")
9          }
10     }()
11 }
```

In the example above, if the send operation cannot proceed within 1 second, the timeout case is selected, effectively preventing the goroutine from blocking indefinitely and thus mitigating the potential for a leak.

Another approach to prevent goroutine leaks involves the judicious use of context cancellation. The context package provides a mechanism to signal goroutines to abort their work and return:

```
1  func contextLeakPreventFunction(ctx context.Context) {
2      ch := make(chan int)
3      go func() {
4          select {
5          case ch <- 42:
6              fmt.Println("Value sent to channel")
```

```
 7        case <-ctx.Done():
 8            fmt.Println("Operation aborted")
 9        }
10    }()
11 }
```

By passing a context with a cancellation function to goroutines and selecting on the <-ctx.Done() case, one can ensure that goroutines terminate gracefully when an operation is no longer needed, hence preventing leaks.

Preventing goroutine leaks is crucial for writing efficient and reliable concurrent Go applications. By employing the select statement with timeouts or context cancellation, developers can ensure that goroutines do not remain blocked indefinitely, thus safeguarding their applications from the performance issues associated with goroutine leaks.

6.9   Order of Case Evaluation in Select

The select statement in Go provides a mechanism for a goroutine to wait on multiple communication operations. A fundamental aspect of using the select statement effectively is understanding the order in which cases are evaluated. This knowledge is crucial for writing predictable and reliable concurrent programs in Go.

When a select statement is executed, if multiple cases can proceed, one case is chosen at random. This stochastic selection process guarantees that no single channel operation is favored over others, promoting fairness and preventing starvation. However, this behavior also means that the program's control flow can vary between executions, depending on the readiness of channel operations.

Consider the following select statement involving multiple channel operations:

```
1  select {
2  case msg1 := <-channel1:
3      fmt.Println("Received", msg1)
4  case msg2 := <-channel2:
5      fmt.Println("Received", msg2)
6  default:
```

```
7       fmt.Println("No message received")
8   }
```

In the example above, if both channel1 and channel2 are ready to send a message, the select statement randomly picks one of the two case blocks to execute. This behavior ensures the program does not consistently favor one channel over another.

To illustrate the non-deterministic nature of case evaluation in a select statement, consider running a program with the above select statement multiple times. Assuming both channels are equally likely to be ready, approximately half of the program executions will print a message from channel1, and the other half will print a message from channel2. The output might appear as follows in different runs:

```
Received message from channel1
Received message from channel2
Received message from channel1
No message received
Received message from channel2
```

Programmers must be aware of this behavior when designing systems that rely on the select statement for concurrency control. Ensuring that your program logic is not dependent on a specific case being selected when multiple cases are ready is essential for the correctness and reliability of your Go applications.

Additionally, the presence of the default case changes the dynamics of case evaluation. The default case is selected only if no other case is ready. This provides a mechanism to perform non-blocking operations when all other channels are unresponsive, allowing programs to avoid deadlock situations and maintain responsiveness.

```
1   select {
2   case msg := <-messages:
3       fmt.Println("Received message", msg)
4   default:
5       fmt.Println("No messages")
6   }
```

In the snippet above, if the messages channel is not ready to send a message, the select statement immediately executes the default case, printing "No messages" and preventing the program from halting indefinitely while waiting for a message.

Understanding the order of case evaluation in the select statement is fundamental when developing concurrent Go applications. By mastering this aspect of the select mechanism, programmers can leverage its full potential to create highly responsive and robust applications.

6.10   Select for Load Balancing

Implementing load balancing in Go applications is crucial for optimizing resource utilization and improving performance. The select statement, when used creatively, enables the development of efficient load balancing mechanisms by distributing tasks across multiple channels.   This approach not only enhances the application's responsiveness but also prevents any single channel from being a bottleneck.

To illustrate how the select statement can be utilized for load balancing, consider an application that processes tasks by sending them to a group of worker goroutines. Each worker has a dedicated task channel. The main goal is to evenly distribute tasks among these workers to ensure an optimal workload distribution.

Begin by defining a simple structure for the task and a function that simulates processing a task:

```go
type Task struct {
    ID int
    Data string
}

// Simulate processing a task
func processTask(task *Task) {
    // Processing code here
}
```

Next, create a worker function. Each worker listens on its own task channel and processes incoming tasks using the processTask function:

```
1  func worker(id int, taskChan <-chan *Task) {
2      for task := range taskChan {
3          fmt.Printf("Worker %d processing task %d\n", id, task.ID)
4          processTask(task)
5      }
6  }
```

With the workers defined, the next step is to implement the load balancing mechanism. This example demonstrates how to use the select statement to distribute tasks across multiple worker channels. Each channel in the select block corresponds to a worker's task channel:

```
1   func distributeTasks(taskChans []chan<- *Task, tasks []*Task) {
2       for _, task := range tasks {
3           select {
4           case taskChans[0] <- task:
5               // Sent to first worker
6           case taskChans[1] <- task:
7               // Sent to second worker
8           // Extend this pattern for more workers
9           default:
10              // Optional: handle the case where all workers are busy
11          }
12      }
13  }
```

This approach ensures that a task is sent to the first available worker. The 'default' case can be used to handle scenarios where all workers are currently busy, which might involve queueing the task or applying backpressure strategies.

However, a limitation of this static implementation is that it does not scale dynamically with the number of workers. To overcome this, a more dynamic approach involves iterating over the channels and selecting one that is ready to receive a task. This requires careful synchronization to prevent race conditions and ensure thread safety.

Through proper application of the select statement for distributing tasks across multiple channels, developers can implement an efficient load balancing mechanism in their Go applications. This not only enhances the application's performance but also leads to a more robust and scalable system design.

6.11   Common Mistakes and Pitfalls

Select statements in Go provide a flexible mechanism for concurrent operations across multiple channels, but misusing them can lead to subtle bugs and performance issues. This section will discuss common mistakes and pitfalls encountered when using select statements in Go, and provide guidance on how to avoid them.

- **Ignoring Select Cases**: A common mistake is not handling all possible select cases, especially when dealing with multiple channels. Ignoring a case can lead to unanticipated behavior or deadlock. It is important to ensure that all relevant cases are covered and appropriately handled.

- **Misunderstanding the Default Case**: The default case in a select statement allows for non-blocking operations. However, misusing the default case can result in a busy-wait loop, leading to high CPU usage. To avoid this, the default case should be used judiciously, typically in combination with a time.Sleep statement to prevent the loop from consuming excessive resources.

```
1  select {
2  case msg := <-messages:
3      fmt.Println("Received message", msg)
4  default:
5      time.Sleep(100 * time.Millisecond)
6  }
```

- **Deadlocks due to Unbuffered Channels**: Using unbuffered channels with select statements in scenarios where both send and receive operations are expected to happen simultaneously can easily lead to a deadlock. To mitigate this, either buffer the channels adequately or ensure that channel operations do not depend on each other in a way that can cause a deadlock.

- **Order of Case Evaluation**: The select statement chooses a case to execute at random if multiple cases are ready. Relying on the order of case evaluation can introduce nondeterminism into the program. Instead of expecting a specific execution order, design the select blocks and corresponding goroutines to handle any order of execution.

```
1  // Misunderstanding order can lead to unexpected behavior
2  select {
3  case <-chan1:
4      // Handle chan1
5  case <-chan2:
6      // Handle chan2
7  }
```

- **Forgetting to Close Channels**: Not closing a channel when it is no longer needed can prevent the garbage collector from re-claiming the goroutines that are blocked waiting on the chan-nel, eventually leading to a goroutine leak. It is crucial to close channels when they are no longer in use.

```
1  func produce(ch chan<- int) {
2      for i := 0; i < 10; i++ {
3          ch <- i
4      }
5      close(ch)
6  }
```

- **Using select with a Single Case**: Using a select statement with only one case, excluding the default case, adds unnecessary complexity to the code. In such situations, a simple send or receive operation on the channel is more appropriate and more readable.

- **Incorrect Timeout Handling**: Improperly handling timeouts with select and time.After can lead to resource leaks, as each call to time.After creates a new timer. To avoid this, it is better to use a time.Ticker for repeated actions, or to stop timers explicitly when they are no longer needed.

```
1  select {
2  case res := <-result:
3      fmt.Println("Received result:", res)
4  case <-time.After(1 * time.Second):
5      fmt.Println("Operation timed out")
6  }
```

Understanding and mitigating these common mistakes and pitfalls when using select statements can lead to more robust and efficient concurrent Go programs. Always consider the implications of each select case, and remember that clarity and simplicity often result in more maintainable code.

6.12   Real-world Applications of Select

The select statement in Go's concurrency model facilitates multiplexed input and output operations through channels. This section discusses several practical scenarios where leveraging the select statement can significantly enhance the capability, responsiveness, and robustness of Go applications.

Chat Server

A common application of the select statement is in the development of a chat server. In this scenario, the server needs to manage multiple client connections, each represented by a channel. The server must listen for incoming messages from all clients and broadcast each message to every client.

```
 1  for {
 2      select {
 3      case msg := <-incomingMessages:
 4          for _, clientChan := range clients {
 5              clientChan <- msg
 6          }
 7      case newClient := <-newClients:
 8          clients = append(clients, newClient)
 9      }
10  }
```

This illustrates how select can be used to concurrently handle a dynamic number of client channels. Incoming messages and new client connections are managed efficiently, with the server reacting to whichever event occurs first.

Implementing Timeouts

Timeouts are crucial for preventing a program from waiting indefinitely on an operation. With the `select` statement, implementing timeouts can be seamlessly integrated into the flow of data operations.

```
select {
case res := <-responseChan:
    process(res)
case <-time.After(10 * time.Second):
    fmt.Println("Operation timed out")
}
```

The `select` statement waits for a response on the `responseChan` channel or for a timeout to occur, whichever happens first. This pattern ensures that the program remains responsive, even in situations where a response might never arrive.

Resource Load Balancer

In systems requiring efficient distribution of tasks among multiple workers, the `select` statement can be employed to implement a simple, yet effective, load balancer. The load balancer can dynamically allocate tasks to workers based on their availability, significantly improving the overall throughput of the system.

```
func balance(workChans []chan Work) {
    var w Work
    var ok bool

    for {
        var sends []selectCase
        for _, ch := range workChans {
            selectCase := reflect.SelectCase{Dir: reflect.SelectSend, Chan:
                reflect.ValueOf(ch), Send: reflect.ValueOf(w)}
            sends = append(sends, selectCase)
        }

        _, _, ok = reflect.Select(sends)
        if !ok {
            break
        }
    }
}
```

By dynamically constructing a slice of `reflect.SelectCase`, this pattern facilitates the distribution of work across available worker channels, enabling efficient task management.

Multiplexing I/O Operations

The ability to wait on multiple I/O operations simultaneously exemplifies the power of the `select` statement. This is particularly useful in network programming, where a server might need to handle multiple clients concurrently without blocking on read or write operations.

```
1   for {
2       select {
3       case data := <-readFromConn1:
4           process(data)
5       case data := <-readFromConn2:
6           process(data)
7       }
8   }
```

This code snippet demonstrates how a server can simultaneously wait for data from two connections, processing data from whichever connection is ready first.

The real-world applications of the `select` statement in Go are vast and varied. By facilitating efficient multiplexing of channel operations, it enables developers to write concurrent applications that are both robust and highly responsive. Whether it's developing a chat server, implementing timeouts, balancing load among workers, or multiplexing I/O operations, the `select` statement proves to be an indispensable tool in the Go concurrency toolkit.

Chapter 7

Context Package for Goroutine Lifecycle Management

The context package in Go provides a framework for managing the lifecycle of goroutines, allowing for graceful cancellation and timeouts, which are essential for building reliable and maintainable concurrent applications. This chapter focuses on how to use the context package effectively, from initiating contexts to propagating them through your application's call stack. It also covers how context can be used to pass critical data across API boundaries, manage deadlines, and handle cancellation signals across concurrently running goroutines. By incorporating context into your Go programs, you can achieve better control over goroutine execution, enhance error handling, and improve the robustness of your applications.

7.1   Introduction to Context in Go

Let's start with an explanation of what context is within the Go programming language. The context package, introduced in Go 1.7, is a powerful yet underutilized feature that provides a means to control the lifecycle of goroutines, which are functions or methods that run concurrently with other functions or methods. Understanding and using context effectively is pivotal for building robust and maintainable concurrent applications.

In concurrent programming, managing the lifecycle of goroutines is crucial. Without proper lifecycle management, programs can leak resources or fail to respond to cancellation signals, leading to unpredictable behavior and performance issues. This is where the context package steps in as a structured way to manage these lifecycle events.

The primary use cases of context in Go include:

- Canceling goroutines: This is a fundamental aspect of managing goroutine lifecycles. The context package allows sending cancellation signals to goroutines, which can then gracefully shut down.

- Setting deadlines: For operations that should be bound by time, context provides a way to set deadlines and automatically cancel operations once the deadlines are exceeded. This is particularly useful for preventing resource leaks in network calls or database queries.

- Value propagation: Context can carry request-scoped values across API boundaries. This is useful for passing data that is relevant to a particular request's execution, like authentication tokens or request identifiers.

To illustrate how context manages goroutine lifecycles, consider the following code snippet that demonstrates a basic use case of context for cancellation:

```
1   package main
```

```
2
3    import (
4        "context"
5        "fmt"
6        "time"
7    )
8
9    func operation(ctx context.Context) {
10       select {
11       case <-time.After(1 * time.Minute):
12           fmt.Println("Operation completed")
13       case <-ctx.Done():
14           fmt.Println("Operation cancelled")
15       }
16   }
17
18   func main() {
19       ctx, cancel := context.WithCancel(context.Background())
20       go operation(ctx)
21
22       time.Sleep(5 * time.Second)
23       cancel()
24   }
```

In this example, the main function initiates a goroutine that performs some operation. The operation listens for a cancellation signal using a select statement. If the cancellation signal is received (via ctx.Done()), the operation prints "Operation cancelled" and returns, thus terminating the goroutine gracefully. The main function waits for 5 seconds before sending the cancellation signal.

Using context for cancelling operations is just the beginning. As this chapter progresses, the versatility and efficacy of the context package in Go's concurrent programming landscape will be further unraveled, encompassing topics such as creating contexts, managing deadlines, handling timeouts, propagating values, and networking patterns sensitive to lifecycle events.

By adopting context in your Go applications, you'll gain finer control over goroutine execution, leading to applications that are both more robust and responsive. The ensuing sections will equip you with the knowledge and practical techniques needed to harness the full potential of the context package, enhancing your concurrent programming skills in Go.

7.2   Using   Context   for   Goroutine Management

The context package in Go facilitates managing the lifecycle of goroutines, ensuring that they can be gracefully cancelled or timed out as required. This capability is foundational for writing robust, concurrent applications that are both resilient and responsive. The effective management of goroutines using the context package involves initiating a context, propagating it through the call stack of the application, and responding appropriately to cancellation signals or deadlines.

To begin, the creation of a context instance is essential. This process usually starts at the highest level of the application, often in the main function or at the start of a new request in a web server. There are two primary context constructors provided by the context package: `context.Background()` and `context.TODO()`. These functions generate a base context which is then used to derive more specific contexts.

```
1  ctx := context.Background()
```

or

```
1  ctx := context.TODO()
```

Once a base context is established, it can be propagated through the application. When a new goroutine is launched, it should receive the context as a parameter. This practice ensures that any goroutine can be notified of cancellation signals or deadlines.

```
1  go func(ctx context.Context) {
2      // Goroutine's work here
3  }(ctx)
```

Cancellation of goroutines is a critical aspect of context use. To initiate a cancellable context, one would use the `context.WithCancel` function. This function returns a copy of the parent context, which can be cancelled by calling the provided cancel function.

184

```
1   ctx, cancel := context.WithCancel(ctx)
```

It is the responsibility of the goroutine to monitor the context's cancellation signal. This is typically done by selecting on the context's Done channel. Once Done is closed, the goroutine should clean up resources and terminate.

```
1   select {
2   case <-ctx.Done():
3       // Clean up and exit the goroutine
4   }
```

In many scenarios, operations need to complete within a certain deadline or timeout. The context package provides the context.WithDeadline and context.WithTimeout functions for these use cases, respectively. Setting a deadline or a timeout returns a context that automatically sends a cancellation signal when the specified time expires.

```
1   ctx, cancel := context.WithTimeout(ctx, 100*time.Millisecond)
```

or

```
1   deadline := time.Now().Add(100 * time.Millisecond)
2   ctx, cancel := context.WithDeadline(ctx, deadline)
```

The use of context in goroutine management enhances the control programmers have over goroutine execution. By leveraging context for cancellation and timeouts, applications can avoid leaking resources and ensure that they remain efficient and responsive under load. Moreover, the ability to pass values through the context enables passing critical data seamlessly across API boundaries without cluttering the function signatures.

The context package's role in managing goroutine lifecycle cannot be overstated. It empowers developers to write concurrent applications that are not only efficient in resource management but also maintainable and robust against the unpredictable nature of executing across multiple threads of execution.

7.3 Creating Contexts: Background and TODO

In this section, we will discuss how to initialize contexts within Go applications, particularly focusing on two primary context constructors: context.Background() and context.TODO(). Understanding these constructors is fundamental for employing the context package to manage goroutine lifecycle effectively.

context.Background()

The context.Background() function returns an empty context. This context is primarily used at the highest level of an application, serving as the root context from which other contexts are derived. It is non-nil, empty, and has no values or deadlines associated with it. The background context is typically used in the main function, initialization functions, and tests, as a base context for the entire application or a significant portion thereof.

The essence of using context.Background() can be demonstrated with a basic example:

```
package main

import (
    "context"
    "fmt"
)

func operation(ctx context.Context) {
    // Simulated operation using the context
    fmt.Println("Performing an operation with context...")
}

func main() {
    ctx := context.Background()
    operation(ctx)
}
```

In this example, context.Background() is employed to instantiate a root context which is then passed to the operation function. This context could be subsequently utilized to derive child contexts or for

186

other context-related functionalities.

context.TODO()

The context.TODO() function also returns a non-nil, empty context, similar to context.Background(). However, the usage semantics of context.TODO() differ significantly. This constructor is intended as a placeholder for contexts in code paths where it is unclear which context to use or during the transitional phase when refactoring code to incorporate context usage. The TODO context signifies that the intention to use context has been acknowledged, but the exact nature of its use has not been determined yet.

An exemplary usage scenario of context.TODO() is illustrated below:

```
package main

import (
    "context"
    "fmt"
)

func uncertainOperation(ctx context.Context) {
    // Operation where the appropriate context to use is yet to be determined
    fmt.Println("Conducting an operation with a TODO context...")
}

func main() {
    ctx := context.TODO()
    uncertainOperation(ctx)
}
```

In the preceding snippet, context.TODO() is utilized to instantiate a context for the uncertainOperation function, highlighting that the choice of context is subject to future determination.

Key Differences

While both context.Background() and context.TODO() create empty context instances, their intended usage scenarios are notably different. context.Background() is suited for initializing the root context in a clear, intended context hierarchy. Conversely, context.TODO() serves as a temporary placeholder during code transition or when the context usage decision is pending.

Utilizing `context.Background()` and `context.TODO()` appropriately within Go applications sets the ground for effective context-based goroutine lifecycle management. These foundational context constructors facilitate the explicit signaling of intent in context usage, paving the way for enhancing code clarity and maintainability.

7.4   Context Values: Passing Data to Goroutines

The ability to pass data between goroutines in a concurrent Go application is critical, especially in complex systems where passing request-scoped data is necessary for operation execution and logging. The context package in Go allows for such data passing without complicating the method signatures or relying on global variables, which can lead to code that is difficult to understand and maintain. This section will focus on how to use context values effectively to pass data to goroutines.

To start, it is important to understand that the context package provides the `context.Context` interface, which carries deadlines, cancellation signals, and other request-scoped values across API boundaries and between processes. While context is predominantly used for cancellation, one of its less discussed but equally important features is its ability to safely transport request-scoped data across goroutine boundaries.

To set a value in a context, you use the `WithValue` function, which returns a copy of the parent context with the new key-value pair added. It's critical to remember that contexts are immutable; hence, `WithValue` does not change the original context but instead returns a new context that carries the added value. Here is how you can set a value:

```
1  ctx := context.Background()
2  ctx = context.WithValue(ctx, "userID", "12345")
```

In the code above, a background context is created using `context.Background()`, and a user ID is attached to it using `context.WithValue`. The key in the context is a value of any type, but it is recommended to define your own types to avoid collisions with keys defined in other packages.

Retrieving a value from a context involves using the `Value` method of the `context.Context` interface. This method accepts a key and returns the corresponding value if it exists; otherwise, it returns `nil`. Here's an example:

```
1  userID := ctx.Value("userID")
2  fmt.Println(userID) // Output: 12345
```

```
12345
```

However, it is important to approach context values with caution. Overuse or misuse can lead to a design that violates the principles of clean architecture, making it hard to trace data flow and dependencies in your application. Here are some guidelines for using context values:

- Use context values only for data that is truly request-scoped and is not part of the function's result.

- Avoid storing critical domain-specific data in context, as it obscures the data flow and makes the code harder to understand.

- When defining keys for context values, use types specific to your package to avoid collisions with other packages.

- Data stored in context is not type-safe, which means it requires type assertion when retrieving. Use type assertions carefully to avoid panics.

In summary, while context values provide a powerful mechanism for passing request-scoped data across goroutine boundaries, they should be used judiciously. When applied correctly, context values can help achieve cleaner, more maintainable concurrent Go applications.

7.5   Cancelling Goroutines with Context

One of the primary utilities of the context package in Go is facilitating the cancellation of goroutines. Goroutines are lightweight threads managed by the Go runtime, and they are a cornerstone of Go's concurrency model. However, managing their lifecycle, especially their termination, is critical for building reliable and resource-efficient applications. This section elucidates how to use context to cancel goroutines effectively, exemplifying the process through code examples and elaborating on its significance.

The context package provides the WithCancel function, which returns a copy of the parent context with a new done channel. The done channel is closed when the cancel function returned by WithCancel is called. Let's consider a simple code example to illustrate this functionality:

```go
package main

import (
    "context"
    "fmt"
    "time"
)

func operation(ctx context.Context) {
    select {
    case <-time.After(5 * time.Second):
        fmt.Println("Operation finished")
    case <-ctx.Done():
        fmt.Println("Operation cancelled")
    }
}

func main() {
    ctx, cancel := context.WithCancel(context.Background())
    go operation(ctx)

    time.Sleep(2 * time.Second)
    cancel()

    time.Sleep(1 * time.Second) // Wait for goroutine to finish
}
```

In the example above, the operation function starts executing a task that is set to finish after 5 seconds. However, it also listens for cancellation signals through the ctx.Done() channel. The main function initializes a context with cancellation capabilities using `context.WithCancel` and starts the `operation` goroutine with this context. After sleeping for 2 seconds, it calls the `cancel` function, which triggers the cancellation signal, causing the `operation` goroutine to terminate prematurely, as evidenced by the printed message "Operation cancelled".

This pattern of cancellation is particularly useful for managing resource cleanup and ensuring that goroutines do not leak system resources. It's crucial for applications that require a high level of responsiveness and reliability.

```
Operation cancelled
```

The output demonstrates that the cancel function effectively terminates the `operation` goroutine before it completes its longer task. This is a fundamental mechanism for managing concurrency in Go, allowing developers to avoid resource leaks and ensure that goroutines respond promptly to termination signals.

To expand on the significance, consider an HTTP server that launches goroutines to handle incoming requests. Without a mechanism to cancel these goroutines, long-running operations could continue indefinitely, consuming resources even after the client has disconnected. By incorporating context cancellation, each operation can be made aware of its cancellation signal, enabling it to terminate gracefully when required.

In summary, understanding and applying context cancellation to goroutines is integral to building robust concurrent applications in Go. It empowers developers to manage resources effectively, enforce timeouts, and ensure that applications remain responsive and efficient under various operational conditions.

7.6   Timeouts and Deadlines with Context

Implementing timeouts and setting deadlines are critical for controlling the execution time of goroutines in Go applications.

This ensures that operations do not hang indefinitely, potentially leading to system resources being unnecessarily occupied. The context package offers mechanisms for both timeouts and deadlines, which when correctly utilized, contribute to the creation of responsive and resilient applications.

To start with timeouts, the context package provides a function context.WithTimeout. This function takes a parent context and a timeout duration as its arguments, returning a derived context (often referred to as the child context) and a cancellation function. The returned context will be automatically cancelled by the system when the specified timeout duration elapses, regardless of the completion status of the operation using this context.

Consider the following example where a timeout is applied to a hypothetical database query operation:

```
 1  func DatabaseQueryWithTimeout(query string) (string, error) {
 2      // Create a context with a timeout of 2 seconds
 3      ctx, cancel := context.WithTimeout(context.Background(), 2*time.Second)
 4      defer cancel() // Ensure the context is cancelled to free resources
 5
 6      resultChannel := make(chan string)
 7      go func() {
 8          // Simulate a database operation
 9          time.Sleep(1*time.Second) // Assume this operation takes 1 second
10          resultChannel <- "Query result"
11      }()
12
13      select {
14      case <-ctx.Done():
15          return "", ctx.Err() // Return the context cancellation error
16      case result := <-resultChannel:
17          return result, nil
18      }
19  }
```

In this example, a channel resultChannel is used to receive the result of a simulated database query operation. Meanwhile, the ctx.Done() channel is monitored for a cancellation signal, which in this case, would be triggered by the timeout. If the timeout occurs before the operation completes, the function returns with an error explaining that the deadline was exceeded.

Moving onto deadlines, the context.WithDeadline function allows for setting a specific point in time by which the context should be cancelled. This is especially useful in scenarios where an operation needs to be completed before a certain deadline regardless of the current time and remaining duration.

The syntax for creating a context with a deadline is shown below:

```
1  deadline := time.Now().Add(5 * time.Minute)
2  ctx, cancel := context.WithDeadline(context.Background(), deadline)
3  defer cancel()
```

This creates a context that will be cancelled 5 minutes from the current time. Like timeouts, contexts with deadlines are crucial in preventing resource leakage and ensuring that operations do not run indefinitely. Both timeouts and deadlines are foundational in managing goroutine lifecycles within Go applications, fostering practices that enhance the resilience and responsiveness of software systems.

To effectively incorporate timeouts and deadlines, it is essential to understand the behavior of the context package and to routinely cancel contexts either explicitly through the cancellation function or by ensuring that all operations respect the cancellation signal. This not only conserves system resources but also improves application performance by preventing unnecessary work.

7.7 Context and Network Operations

Incorporating context into network operations significantly enhances the reliability and responsiveness of Go applications. Network requests—whether they are HTTP requests to web servers, database queries, or calls to remote procedure calls (RPCs)—inherently possess uncertainty in their execution time. This uncertainty can stem from network latency, server load, or resource contention. The use of context in these scenarios enables setting deadlines, managing timeouts, and providing an avenue for request cancellation, thereby offering a mechanism to avoid blocking goroutines indefinitely and ensuring resource cleanup after the termination of operations.

Setting Deadlines for HTTP Requests

When executing HTTP requests, it's crucial to not allow these requests to continue indefinitely in case of network issues or unresponsive servers, as this can lead to goroutine leaks and wasted resources.   The context package allows developers to specify a deadline for these requests. Below is an example of how to apply deadlines to HTTP requests using context.

```
package main

import (
    "context"
    "net/http"
    "time"
)

func main() {
    ctx, cancel := context.WithDeadline(context.Background(), time.Now().Add(2*
        time.Second))
    defer cancel() // Ensure that resource is cleaned up

    req, _ := http.NewRequestWithContext(ctx, "GET", "http://example.com", nil)
    client := &http.Client{}
    response, err := client.Do(req)
    if err != nil {
        // Handle error
        panic(err)
    }
    defer response.Body.Close()
    // Process response
}
```

In this example, the context with a deadline is created using `context.WithDeadline`, with a deadline of 2 seconds from the current time. This context is then attached to the HTTP request. If the server does not respond within 2 seconds, the request is automatically cancelled.

Handling Timeouts in Database Operations

Database operations can also benefit from context to manage operation timeouts. Most modern Go database drivers support context, allowing developers to specify how long a database call may take before it is considered failed and aborted. Here's an exemplary usage with a database query:

```
1   package main
2
3   import (
4       "context"
5       "database/sql"
6       "log"
7       "time"
8
9       _ "github.com/lib/pq" // Example for PostgreSQL driver
10  )
11
12  func main() {
13      db, err := sql.Open("postgres", "your_connection_string")
14      if err != nil {
15          log.Fatal(err)
16      }
17
18      ctx, cancel := context.WithTimeout(context.Background(), 1*time.Second)
19      defer cancel()
20
21      var name string
22      err = db.QueryRowContext(ctx, "SELECT name FROM users WHERE id=1").Scan(&name
            )
23      if err != nil {
24          log.Fatal(err)
25      }
26
27      log.Println("Retrieved name:", name)
28  }
```

This code snippet features the use of `context.WithTimeout` to set a maximum duration of 1 second for the database query to be completed. If the query execution exceeds this duration, it's automatically cancelled, preventing the application from hanging indefinitely due to database slowness or unavailability.

Cancellation Signals in Long-Running Network Operations

In situations where network operations are expected to run for an extended duration but may need to be terminated prematurely (e.g., user-initiated cancellations in a web application), context can be used to propagate cancellation signals. Here is a skeleton code demonstrating this pattern:

```
1   package main
```

```
2
3   import (
4       "context"
5       "fmt"
6       "time"
7   )
8
9   func longRunningOperation(ctx context.Context) {
10      select {
11      case <-time.After(5 * time.Second):
12          fmt.Println("Operation completed")
13      case <-ctx.Done():
14          fmt.Println("Operation cancelled")
15      }
16  }
17
18  func main() {
19      ctx, cancel := context.WithCancel(context.Background())
20      go longRunningOperation(ctx)
21
22      time.Sleep(2 * time.Second) // Simulate doing other work
23      cancel() // Cancel the operation
24
25      time.Sleep(1 * time.Second) // Wait to see the cancellation effect
26  }
```

In this sample, a hypothetical long-running network operation is initiated as a goroutine. The main function simulates a scenario where, after some time (2 seconds), a decision is made to cancel the operation, which is then communicated through the ctx.Done() channel. The goroutine checks this channel and terminates early, demonstrating a responsive cancellation mechanism that can be leveraged in more complex network operations to manage resources effectively and maintain application responsiveness.

By leveraging the context package in network operations, Go developers can gain fine-grained control over request execution, ensuring that their applications are resilient, responsive, and efficient in their resource use.

7.8   Best Practices for Using Context

To effectively use the context package in Go for managing the lifecycle of goroutines, several best practices should be followed. These guidelines facilitate the development of reliable, maintainable, and robust concurrent applications.

Derive Contexts Whenever Possible

It is essential to create new contexts by deriving from existing ones rather than starting from the context.Background() or context.TODO() in every situation. Deriving contexts helps maintain the hierarchy and lifecycle of goroutine executions. For instance, when initiating a web request handler, start with a base context and derive child contexts for individual operations:

```
1  func handler(w http.ResponseWriter, r *http.Request) {
2      ctx := context.Background()
3      childCtx, cancel := context.WithCancel(ctx)
4      defer cancel()
5
6      // Pass childCtx to operations
7  }
```

Cancellation Propagation

The cancellation mechanism in the context package ensures that all goroutines participating in an operation can be notified when the operation is no longer needed. To leverage this mechanism effectively, ensure that any function that starts a goroutine takes context as its first parameter and observes its cancellation signal:

```
1  func operation(ctx context.Context) {
2      select {
3      case <- ctx.Done():
4          // Handle cancellation
5          return
6      case result := <- someOperation():
7          // Proceed with result
8      }
9  }
```

Timeouts and Deadlines

Apply deadlines or timeouts to contexts only when necessary, and prefer deadlines over timeouts for operations with a clear end time.

Use context.WithDeadline() for setting a specific point in time after which the context will be cancelled, and context.WithTimeout() for specifying a duration:

```
ctx, cancel := context.WithTimeout(context.Background(), 5*time.Second)
defer cancel()
```

Do Not Pass Contexts in Structs

Contexts are meant to be passed through your application's call stack, not stored in structs. "Storing" a context inside a struct can lead to misuse and difficulties in understanding the lifespan and relationships between different contexts and goroutines. Always pass contexts explicitly to functions where they are needed:

```
// Avoid
type MyStruct struct {
    ctx context.Context
}

// Prefer
func (m *MyStruct) Operation(ctx context.Context) {
    // Implementation
}
```

Minimal Context Values

The context.WithValue() function allows passing request-scoped values across API boundaries. However, overuse of context values can lead to obscure code and potential memory leaks. Always aim to pass values explicitly through parameters when possible and reserve context values for truly request-scoped data:

```
ctx := context.WithValue(context.Background(), key, "value")
```

Follow Context Propagation Patterns

Adhering to standard patterns for context propagation ensures consistency across your application. One common pattern is the "incoming requests with outgoing calls" pattern, where a new context for an inbound request is immediately created and used for all outgoing calls made while processing that request. This pattern ensures that cancellation and timeout signals are correctly propagated throughout the call chain.

Testing with Contexts

When writing tests for your Go applications, it's crucial to include tests that simulate the cancellation and deadline exceeding scenarios. This ensures that your application responds correctly to these signals in real-world conditions. Use the `context.WithCancel()` and `context.WithDeadline()` functions to create contexts with cancellation and deadlines in your tests.

Following these best practices enables developers to utilize the `context` package in Go effectively, ensuring that applications are maintainable, efficient, and resilient against common concurrency issues.

7.9 Context Propagation Patterns

In concurrent programming with Go, understanding and implementing efficient context propagation patterns is crucial for creating resilient and scalable applications. Context propagation refers to the process of passing a context from one goroutine to another, throughout the application's call stack. This section delineates several patterns for context propagation, emphasizing their applicability in different scenarios.

The Thread-Per-Request Pattern

One of the simplest and most straightforward patterns is the "Thread-Per-Request" model, often employed in web servers and API handlers. Here, a new goroutine is spawned for each incoming request, and the context is passed to this goroutine at the moment of creation.

```
1   func handler(w http.ResponseWriter, r *http.Request) {
2       ctx := r.Context()
3       go processRequest(ctx)
4   }
5
6   func processRequest(ctx context.Context) {
7       // Implementation
8   }
```

This pattern ensures that each request is handled independently, with its cancellation or timeout signals appropriately isolated. It exemplifies how context can be effectively propagated at the very start of a request's lifecycle.

The Fan-Out/Fan-In Pattern

Another prevalent pattern is the "Fan-Out/Fan-In" model, where a task is divided among multiple goroutines (fan-out), and their results are subsequently aggregated (fan-in). When employing this pattern, context is passed to each goroutine involved in the fan-out stage, ensuring that cancellation or deadline signals are respected across all concurrent operations.

```
1    func processWithFanOutFanIn(ctx context.Context, data []Data) Result {
2        var wg sync.WaitGroup
3        results := make(chan Result, len(data))
4
5        for _, d := range data {
6            wg.Add(1)
7            go func(d Data) {
8                defer wg.Done()
9                if result, err := processPiece(ctx, d); err == nil {
10                   results <- result
11               }
12           }(d)
13       }
14
15       go func() {
16           wg.Wait()
17           close(results)
18       }()
19
20       finalResult := aggregateResults(results)
21       return finalResult
22   }
```

The advantage of this pattern is its ability to handle complex tasks in a parallel, yet controlled manner. It leverages the context to manage the lifecycle of multiple concurrent operations effectively.

Context With Values: Propagating Metadata

Context can also be used to propagate request-specific metadata across an application's call stack, aside from handling cancellation and timeouts. This is particularly useful in tracing and monitoring operations, allowing metadata, such as request IDs or user information, to be accessible in deeply nested function calls.

```
1   func startOperation(ctx context.Context) {
2       requestId := ctx.Value("requestId").(string)
3       log.Printf("Starting operation for request ID: %s", requestId)
4       // Further processing
5   }
```

However, it's crucial to use this feature judiciously, as over-reliance on context values for passing critical function parameters can lead to less readable and maintainable code. It's recommended to limit the use of context values to metadata that is relevant across function boundaries where passing through function parameters would be impractical.

Best Practices for Context Propagation

Finally, a few best practices can ensure effective and efficient context propagation:

- Always propagate context by passing it as the first argument to a function.

- Avoid storing ctx in structs or globally to prevent improper usage or leaks.

- Use `context.WithTimeout` and `context.WithDeadline` judiciously to prevent unnecessary system load or premature cancellations.

- Keep context values light; don't use them to pass around large or critical data structures crucial for function execution.

Understanding and applying these context propagation patterns and practices can significantly enhance the robustness, readability, and maintainability of Go applications dealing with concurrent operations. It enables developers to write more resilient and performance-oriented code by managing goroutine lifecycles more effectively.

7.10   Context in Web Servers and API Calls

In the domain of web servers and API calls, the context package in Go has emerged as a pivotal tool for managing request lifecycles and passing data through the various layers of an application. This section elucidates the integration of context within these environments, underscoring its significance and demonstrating its practical application through code examples.

The integration of context in web server handlers allows for the management of request-scoped values, cancellation signals, and deadlines across API boundaries. This is essential in ensuring that long-running requests do not exhaust system resources and that the server remains responsive even under heavy load.

Incorporating Context into HTTP Handlers

The `net/http` package in Go's standard library provides built-in support for contexts within HTTP requests. Each request is accompanied by a context, accessible via the `Request.Context()` method. This context is automatically cancelled when the client closes the connection, enabling the server to terminate any associated processing.

Consider the following example, which demonstrates how to incorporate context into a basic HTTP handler:

```go
package main

import (
    "fmt"
    "net/http"
    "time"
)

func handler(w http.ResponseWriter, r *http.Request) {
    ctx := r.Context()
    fmt.Println("Server processing request")

    select {
    case <-time.After(5 * time.Second):
        fmt.Fprintln(w, "Request processed")
    case <-ctx.Done():
        err := ctx.Err()
        fmt.Println("Server request cancelled:", err)
    }
}

func main() {
    http.HandleFunc("/", handler)
    http.ListenAndServe(":8080", nil)
}
```

In this example, the handler initiates a processing operation simulated by a 5-second timer. The select statement listens for completion of this operation or cancellation of the context. If the client cancels the request (e.g., closing the browser), the server detects this through the context and terminates the processing early.

Passing Contexts in API Calls

When making outbound API calls from your server, it is crucial to propagate the request context to these external calls. This ensures that if the initial HTTP request to your server is cancelled, any ongoing API calls made as part of processing this request can also be cancelled, thereby conserving resources and preventing unnecessary processing.

Here is an example of passing context to an HTTP client call:

```go
func makeAPICall(ctx context.Context, url string) (string, error) {
    req, err := http.NewRequestWithContext(ctx, "GET", url, nil)
    if err != nil {
        return "", err
```

```
5        }
6
7        resp, err := http.DefaultClient.Do(req)
8        if err != nil {
9            return "", err
10       }
11       defer resp.Body.Close()
12
13       body, err := ioutil.ReadAll(resp.Body)
14       if err != nil {
15           return "", err
16       }
17
18       return string(body), nil
19   }
```

In this function, http.NewRequestWithContext is used to create a new HTTP request attached with the provided context. This ensures that if the context is cancelled, the HTTP client request is also aborted.

Best Practices

When integrating context in web servers and API calls, adhere to the following best practices:

- Always pass the context as the first parameter in functions.

- Do not store context within a struct; pass it explicitly wherever needed.

- Initiate a new context with context.Background() only in the main function or when starting a new goroutine.

- Avoid putting sensitive information into context values, as they can be accessed by any part of your application.

By adhering to these practices and effectively utilizing context in web servers and API calls, developers can enhance the resilience and maintainability of their Go applications, ensuring that resources are used judiciously and that applications remain responsive and robust under varying load conditions.

7.11   Common Mistakes with Context

The use of the context package in Go is accompanied by certain common pitfalls that can undermine the effectiveness of its implementation and the robustness of the application. Identifying and avoiding these mistakes is crucial for developers striving to manage goroutine lifecycles efficiently and maintain the integrity of concurrent operations. This section outlines the most commonly encountered missteps and provides guidance on how to avoid them.

1. Ignoring Cancellation Signals

One of the primary functions of the context package is to propagate cancellation signals to goroutines. A common mistake is to ignore these signals, which can lead to goroutines that continue to run even after they have been instructed to terminate, thereby consuming system resources unnecessarily.

```
func operation(ctx context.Context) {
    // Incorrect: Ignoring the ctx.Done() channel
    heavyComputation()
    // Proper handling requires checking the ctx.Done() channel
}
```

2. Misusing Background and TODO Contexts

The `context.Background()` and `context.TODO()` functions are intended for specific use cases. Misusing these contexts can lead to confusion and difficulties in managing goroutine lifecycles effectively.

- `context.Background()` should be used as the top-level context for main and init functions, serving as the root of all derived contexts.

- `context.TODO()` is intended for placeholders where future context integration is planned but not yet implemented.

3. Overuse of Context Values

Storing excessive amounts of data within the context can lead to overcomplicated code and difficulties in managing and accessing the stored data effectively.

```
1   ctx = context.WithValue(ctx, "key", "excessive use of context values")
```

Optimally, context values should be limited to data that is essential for across-boundary API calls and goroutine execution control.

4. Creating Too Many Contexts

Creating a new context for every single function call, regardless of whether it is necessary, can lead to a proliferation of context instances that are difficult to trace and manage.

```
1   func unnecessaryContextCreation() {
2       ctx := context.WithCancel(context.Background())
3       // Creating a new context here might not be necessary
4   }
```

5. Failing to Propagate Context

Failing to pass the context down the call stack is a critical mistake that can prevent cancellation signals from reaching goroutines further down the hierarchy, leading to unresponsive or hanging goroutines.

```
1   func doSomething(ctx context.Context) {
2       // Incorrect: not passing ctx to the next function call
3       result := nextOperation()
4   }
```

6. Incorrect Usage of Contexts in Goroutines

When launching new goroutines, it's essential to pass the appropriate context to them. Ignoring this can result in goroutines that do not respond to cancellation or timeout signals.

```
1  go func() {
2      // Incorrect: New goroutine not receiving any context
3      performAction()
4  }()
```

Avoiding these common mistakes requires a thorough understanding of the context package and its proper use within Go applications. Developers should strive to use context judiciously, respecting its role in managing the lifecycle of goroutines and ensuring the efficient execution of concurrent operations.

7.12 Advanced Techniques with Context

Let's delve into some advanced techniques that leverage the Context package in Go to manage the lifecycle of goroutines. These techniques go beyond basic cancellations and deadlines, offering patterns that could significantly enhance the utility and manageability of concurrent operations within Go applications.

Dynamically Adjusting Context Deadlines

At times, the fixed timeout period for a context isn't sufficient or optimal. Situations might arise necessitating the extension or reduction of deadlines based on dynamic run-time conditions. To achieve such flexibility, one can use the initial context to derive new ones with adjusted deadlines.

```
1  ctx, cancel := context.WithTimeout(context.Background(), 10 * time.
       Second)
2  defer cancel()
3
4  // Dynamically decide that more time is needed
5  var needMoreTime bool
6  // This value would typically result from some runtime conditions
7  if needMoreTime {
8      // Extend the deadline by 5 more seconds
9      var extendedDeadline = time.Now().Add(5 * time.Second)
10     ctx, cancel = context.WithDeadline(ctx, extendedDeadline)
11     defer cancel()
```

```
12 }
```

This example illustrates how to dynamically adjust the deadline of a context. It's important to defer the cancellation of the newly created context to ensure resources are released properly.

Using Context for Selective Goroutine Cancellation

In complex applications, it's common to spawn multiple goroutines that may need to be selectively cancelled instead of employing a blanket cancellation. Utilizing context trees is a sophisticated method to achieve this.

```
1  parentCtx, parentCancel := context.WithCancel(context.Background())
2  defer parentCancel()
3
4  childCtx1, cancel1 := context.WithCancel(parentCtx)
5  defer cancel1()
6
7  childCtx2, cancel2 := context.WithCancel(parentCtx)
8  defer cancel2()
9
10 go func(ctx context.Context) {
11     // operation for childCtx1
12 }(childCtx1)
13
14 go func(ctx context.Context) {
15     // operation for childCtx2
16 }(childCtx2)
17
18 // Cancel childCtx1 selectively
19 cancel1()
```

In this pattern, child contexts are derived from a common parent. By cancelling a specific child context, the associated goroutines can be terminated without affecting others in the hierarchy. This practice allows for granular control over goroutine cancellation.

Context with Value Propagation for Tracing

The propagation of request-specific data across API boundaries and throughout the concurrency model of an application can be elegantly handled with context values. This is particularly useful for tracing and monitoring purposes.

```
1  ctx := context.WithValue(context.Background(), "RequestID", "123456")
2  go func(ctx context.Context) {
3      requestID := ctx.Value("RequestID")
4      fmt.Println("Handling request with ID:", requestID)
5  }(ctx)
```

While utilizing context.WithValue is convenient for passing data, it's crucial to use this feature judiciously to avoid cluttering context objects with unnecessary data or causing reliance on context values for critical operations, which could lead to brittle design.

Integrating Context with Channel Operations

In asynchronous operations that rely on channels for signaling completion or passing data, context can be integrated to add cancellation capability.

```
1  ctx, cancel := context.WithCancel(context.Background())
2  defer cancel()
3
4  doneChan := make(chan struct{})
5
6  go func() {
7      select {
8      case <-ctx.Done():
9          fmt.Println("Operation cancelled")
10     case <-doneChan:
11         fmt.Println("Operation completed successfully")
12     }
13 }()
```

This demonstrates how a goroutine can listen for both cancellation signals through the context and operation completion signals through a channel, allowing for more expressive and flexible concurrent operation handling.

Through these advanced techniques, developers can leverage the Context package in Go not only for cancellation and timeouts but also for sophisticated lifecycle management, propagation of request-specific data, and integration with Go's concurrency patterns such as channels. These patterns significantly contribute to writing concurrent Go applications that are both robust and maintainable.

Chapter 8

Testing and Benchmarking Concurrent Code

Testing and benchmarking are critical components of developing reliable and efficient concurrent applications in Go. This chapter covers strategies and tools provided by Go for testing concurrent code, including the detection of race conditions and the benchmarking of concurrent functions to assess performance. It also delves into best practices for writing testable concurrent applications, such as mocking concurrent dependencies and integrating concurrency tests into continuous integration pipelines. By applying these techniques, developers can ensure that their Go applications are not only concurrent but also correct and performant, ready to handle the demands of real-world usage.

8.1   Introduction   to   Testing   and Benchmarking

Testing and benchmarking serve as foundational pillars for developing robust and high-performance concurrent applications in Go. Effective testing ensures the correctness of the application under various conditions, while benchmarking evaluates its performance, specifically how fast and efficiently it operates. This dual approach is particularly vital for concurrent programming, where the interplay between multiple threads or goroutines can introduce complex behaviors and performance characteristics not present in sequential code.

Let's start with an understanding of why testing concurrent code demands a different strategy compared to testing sequential code. In concurrent applications, components often run simultaneously, potentially accessing shared resources in an environment that is inherently unpredictable. This unpredictability means that issues such as race conditions, deadlocks, and non-deterministic behavior can be more challenging to identify and resolve. Therefore, tests designed for concurrent applications need to account for these complexities to ensure comprehensive coverage.

Regarding benchmarking, it provides a quantifiable measure of an application's performance, specifically looking into aspects such as runtime, memory consumption, and CPU usage. When applied to concurrent code, benchmarking helps to identify bottlenecks and inefficiencies that could degrade the application's overall performance. For instance, a poorly designed concurrent algorithm might lead to excessive context switching or contention over shared resources, both of which can significantly impact execution speed and resource utilization.

The Go programming language comes equipped with tools and methodologies tailored for these tasks. The testing package, for example, includes support for writing unit tests, benchmarking functions, and spotting race conditions through the command line flag -race. These tools, when used effectively, empower developers to write, test, and optimize concurrent Go applications with confidence.

A critical aspect of testing concurrent code is to simulate and test against a broad range of conditions to account for the non-deterministic nature of concurrency. This might involve tests that force goroutines to execute in a particular order, or the introduction of artificial delays to uncover hidden race conditions.

On the benchmarking front, Go's benchmarking mechanism allows developers to measure the time it takes for a function to execute, facilitating the comparison between different concurrency strategies or optimization efforts. It is crucial, however, to ensure that benchmark tests are repeatable and cover realistic use cases to provide meaningful insights into the application's performance.

Finally, both testing and benchmarking should be integrated into a continuous integration (CI) pipeline. This integration ensures that every code change is automatically tested and benchmarked against predefined metrics, helping to maintain and improve code quality throughout the development lifecycle.

In summary, mastering testing and benchmarking techniques is indispensable for developing high-quality concurrent applications in Go. By delving into the strategies and tools available for testing and optimizing concurrent code, developers can ensure their applications are both correct and performant.

8.2 Writing Unit Tests for Concurrent Functions

When developing concurrent applications in Go, unit testing plays a pivotal role in ensuring code reliability and correctness. Given the inherent complexities of concurrent programming, such as potential race conditions and deadlocks, writing effective unit tests for concurrent functions requires a methodical approach.

Understanding Go's Testing Framework

The Go programming language provides a comprehensive testing package, which is utilized for writing unit tests. To write a unit test for a concurrent function, one starts by creating a new .go file with a naming convention that ends in _test.go. Tests are written in functions that start with the word Test followed by the function name, and accepts a pointer to testing.T as its only parameter.

```
1  func TestMyConcurrentFunction(t *testing.T) {
2      // Test body
3  }
```

This structure is the foundation for writing any test in Go, including those for concurrent functions.

Initiating Multiple Goroutines

Testing concurrent functionality often requires initiating multiple goroutines within your test to mimic concurrent execution. This can be exemplified when testing a function designed to perform operations in parallel.

```
1  func TestParallelExecution(t *testing.T) {
2      done := make(chan bool)
3      go func() {
4          // Call your concurrent function here
5          done <- true
6      }()
7      <-done // Wait for the goroutine to finish
8  }
```

The above example demonstrates a simple method to wait for a concurrently executing function by utilizing a channel. However, for more complex scenarios involving multiple goroutines, synchronization techniques such as WaitGroup can be employed.

Employing sync.WaitGroup for Synchronization

The sync.WaitGroup is invaluable when managing multiple goroutines within your tests. It allows you to wait for all goroutines that have been added to the WaitGroup to complete their execution before continuing.

```
1   func TestMultipleGoroutines(t *testing.T) {
2       var wg sync.WaitGroup
3       wg.Add(2) // Number of goroutines to wait for
4
5       go func() {
6           defer wg.Done()
7           // First concurrent operation
8       }()
9
10      go func() {
11          defer wg.Done()
12          // Second concurrent operation
13      }()
14
15      wg.Wait() // Block until all goroutines are done
16  }
```

This approach ensures that your test only passes if all concurrent operations have completed, thus preventing false positives that might occur due to the asynchronous nature of concurrent execution.

Using Channels for Inter-Goroutine Communication

Channels are a core component of concurrent programming in Go, facilitating communication between goroutines. When testing functions that involve inter-goroutine communication, channels can also be used to synchronize and pass data between the test and the goroutines.

```
1   func TestChannelCommunication(t *testing.T) {
2       messages := make(chan string)
3       go func() {
4           messages <- "ping"
5       }()
6       msg := <-messages
7       if msg != "ping" {
8           t.Errorf("Expected 'ping', got '%s'", msg)
9       }
10  }
```

This example demonstrates a test for a goroutine sending a string message through a channel. The test verifies the message sent by the goroutine, illustrating a simple pattern for testing channel-based communication.

Handling Race Conditions

One of the challenges in testing concurrent code is detecting and handling race conditions. Go's testing framework offers the -race flag, which can be used when running tests to detect race conditions automatically.

```
go test -race mypackage
```

The race detector is a powerful tool for identifying race conditions in your code, including those within concurrent tests. It should be used regularly as part of your testing strategy to ensure the safety and reliability of your concurrent functions.

Writing unit tests for concurrent functions in Go requires consideration of the concurrent behavior being tested. By effectively employing goroutines, channels, synchronization techniques, and race condition detection, developers can create robust tests that ensure the correct operation of concurrent code. The strategies outlined in this section provide a foundation for developing comprehensive tests for concurrent applications in Go.

8.3   Using   Go's   Testing   Package   for Concurrency

Go's standard library includes a powerful testing package, referred to as testing, designed to facilitate the creation, execution, and analysis of unit and benchmark tests. This section will focus on leveraging the testing package to test concurrent code effectively. Concurrent programming introduces complexities not seen in sequential code, notably issues related to timing, state management, and resource sharing. Therefore, testing concurrent applications requires a thoughtful approach to ensure that the software behaves as expected under various conditions.

To illustrate the usage of the `testing` package for concurrency, let's start with the basic structure of a test function in Go. A test function takes a pointer to `testing.T` as its only parameter. This object provides methods for reporting test failures and logging additional information.

```
func TestMyConcurrentFunction(t *testing.T) {
    // Test body
}
```

In the context of concurrent applications, our focus is on testing the behavior of go routines and their interactions. One common approach is to launch multiple goroutines within the test function and use synchronization mechanisms, such as channels or wait groups, to orchestrate the concurrent operations.

Let's consider a scenario where we have a function `ProcessDataConcurrently` that launches several goroutines to process data in parallel. To test this function, we might want to ensure that it correctly aggregates the results from all goroutines.

```
func TestProcessDataConcurrently(t *testing.T) {
    result := ProcessDataConcurrently()
    expected := 42 // Assuming we expect the result to be 42

    if result != expected {
        t.Errorf("Expected %d, got %d", expected, result)
    }
}
```

An essential aspect of testing concurrent code is dealing with indeterminism. The execution order of goroutines is not guaranteed, leading to flaky tests if not handled correctly. One strategy to mitigate this is to use synchronization mechanisms or to introduce controlled delays (though the latter should be used sparingly and carefully).

Next, let's explore how to use the `testing` package for benchmarking concurrent functions. Benchmark tests in Go are designed to measure the performance of code. These tests are particularly important for concurrent applications where performance is a key concern.

```
func BenchmarkMyConcurrentFunction(b *testing.B) {
    for i := 0; i < b.N; i++ {
        // Call the concurrent function here
```

```
4        }
5    }
```

The `testing.B` object provides the N field, which tells your benchmark code how many times to run the benchmarked code. The Go testing framework automatically determines N to get a reliable measurement.

When benchmarking concurrent code, it's crucial to consider the setup and tear-down times that might disproportionately affect the measurement for fast operations. Moreover, it's vital to ensure that the benchmark does not inadvertently test system synchronization (e.g., locking mechanisms) rather than the code's logic.

Go's `testing` package offers a robust framework for testing and benchmarking concurrent applications. By carefully structuring tests and making thoughtful use of Go's concurrency primitives within tests, developers can significantly enhance the reliability and performance of their concurrent Go applications. As with all concurrency-related development, attentiveness to the unique challenges posed by concurrent execution—such as synchronization, ordering, and shared state management—is paramount.

8.4   Benchmarking Concurrent Code with Go

Benchmarking is a quantitative approach that measures the performance of code under particular circumstances. Specifically, for concurrent applications developed in Go, benchmarking evaluates how effectively the application utilizes system resources, such as CPU and memory, under varying levels of concurrency.

The Benchmark Function

In Go, a benchmark function is defined similarly to a test function, but it takes a `*testing.B` parameter and is named with a `Benchmark` prefix. This parameter provides the infrastructure for running a function repeatedly and measuring its performance. It is crucial that the benchmark function is carefully designed to avoid compiler optimizations that could eliminate the function under test.

```
func BenchmarkConcurrentFunction(b *testing.B) {
    for i := 0; i < b.N; i++ {
        ConcurrentFunction()
    }
}
```

In this example, ConcurrentFunction is called repeatedly within a loop that executes b.N times. The testing package dynamically adjusts the value of b.N to ensure the benchmark runs long enough to produce reliable metrics.

Running Benchmarks

To run benchmarks, the go test command is utilized with the -bench flag, targeting the specific benchmark function or functions.

```
go test -bench=BenchmarkConcurrentFunction
```

This command will execute the benchmark defined by BenchmarkConcurrentFunction and report the time taken per operation. The output provides insights into the efficiency of the concurrent function, highlighting potential areas for optimization.

Measuring Resources

In addition to time per operation, it is often valuable to measure other resources like memory allocation and CPU cycles. The Go testing package provides benchmarking flags, such as -benchmem, to collect this data.

```
go test -bench=BenchmarkConcurrentFunction -benchmem
```

This command will output not only the time per operation but also the bytes per operation and allocations per operation, providing a comprehensive view of the function's performance.

Analyzing Concurrency

A unique aspect of benchmarking concurrent code is the need to understand how performance scales with concurrency. For this, Go benchmarks can be parameterized to run the same test under different concurrency levels.

```go
func BenchmarkConcurrentFunctionWithGoroutines(b *testing.B) {
    for _, n := range []int{1, 2, 4, 8, 16} {
        b.Run(fmt.Sprintf("Goroutines=%d", n), func(b *testing.B) {
            for i := 0; i < b.N; i++ {
                ConcurrentFunctionWithN(n)
            }
        })
    }
}
```

In this code snippet, `ConcurrentFunctionWithN` is executed with varying numbers of goroutines, enabling the evaluation of how adding more concurrency impacts performance. Benchmark results for each level of concurrency provide invaluable data for tuning concurrent applications.

Benchmarking concurrent code in Go is pivotal for optimizing performance and resource utilization. By employing Go's testing package to write and run benchmarks, and analyzing the data collected, developers can make informed decisions about concurrency patterns and resource allocation, ultimately enhancing the efficiency of their concurrent applications.

This section has detailed the process for devising and executing benchmarks in Go, specifically focusing on concurrent code. Understanding these techniques is essential for developing performant and resource-efficient Go applications that are capable of meeting the demands of scalable, real-world usage.

8.5   Race Detection in Tests

Detecting race conditions in concurrent programming is paramount for ensuring the correctness and reliability of applications. Go provides a built-in race detector that can be utilized during tests to automatically identify race conditions. This section elucidates the process of employing the race detector in Go tests, alongside interpreting its results for effective debugging.

To enable the race detector in your tests, the -race flag must be passed to the go test command. This instructs Go's compiler and runtime to observe accesses to shared variables during the test execution and report any race conditions detected. Consider the following example where a test is run with the race detector enabled:

```
1   go test -race ./...
```

When a race condition is detected, the output will contain details about the conflict, including the involved goroutines and the exact lines of code accessing the shared resource concurrently. An exemplar output may look as follows:

```
==================
WARNING: DATA RACE
Read at 0x00c0000b8008 by goroutine 8:
  runtime.slicecopy()
      /usr/local/go/src/runtime/slice.go:197 +0x0
  main.main.func1()
      /path/to/your/package/main.go:25 +0x9a

Previous write at 0x00c0000b8008 by goroutine 7:
  main.main()
      /path/to/your/package/main.go:20 +0x88

Goroutine 8 (running) created at:
  main.main()
      /path/to/your/package/main.go:24 +0x78

Goroutine 7 (finished) created at:
  main.main()
      /path/to/your/package/main.go:19 +0x60
==================
```

Interpreting the race detector's output involves identifying the conflicting operations (reads/writes) and the code locations where they occur. The output meticulously outlines each operation, pinpointing the source lines and the respective goroutines involved. This information is invaluable for tracing back and remedying the concurrency issue.

In practice, it is recommended to:

- Regularly run tests with the -race flag during the development cycle to catch and fix race conditions early.

- Employ the race detector in continuous integration (CI) pipelines to ensure race conditions are detected before code merges into the main branch.

It is important to note, however, that enabling the race detector incurs a performance penalty during test execution. This stems from the additional checks and monitoring required to detect concurrent accesses to shared resources. Consequently, test execution times will be noticeably longer when the race detector is active. Despite this, the benefits of early detection of race conditions far outweigh the temporary inconvenience of extended test durations.

Lastly, while the Go race detector is a powerful tool for identifying race conditions, it is not infallible. It can only detect races that actually occur during test runs. Thus, absence of warnings from the race detector does not guarantee the non-existence of race conditions. Complementary strategies, including thorough code reviews and designing with concurrency best practices in mind, are essential for minimizing the likelihood of race conditions in your Go applications.

8.6   Strategies for Mocking Concurrent Dependencies

Testing concurrent applications presents unique challenges, as tests need to account for the non-deterministic nature of concurrent execution. A critical technique in addressing these challenges is the mocking of concurrent dependencies. This strategy involves simulating the behavior of complex, real-world components that a piece of code depends on, allowing for controlled and deterministic tests. This section discusses several strategies for effectively mocking concurrent dependencies in Go.

Understanding the Need for Mocking

Before delving into specific strategies, it is essential to understand why mocking is particularly important in the context of concurrent programming. Concurrency introduces a level of complexity and unpredictability due to the simultaneous execution of code. As such, testing concurrent code requires isolating the unit of work from its concurrent dependencies to ensure that the tests are deterministic and reliable. Mocking serves as a tool to achieve this isolation by replacing these dependencies with controllable and predictable versions.

Using Interfaces to Mock Dependencies

One of the foundational strategies in Go for mocking dependencies is through the use of interfaces. Interfaces in Go provide a way to define a contract for the behavior of an object without specifying its implementation. This characteristic makes them an excellent tool for mocking, as they allow developers to create mock implementations that fulfill the interface contract but contain controlled, predictable behavior for testing.

Consider a simple example where a concurrent function interacts with a database. To test this function without hitting an actual database, one can define an interface that describes the database interaction and then implement a mock database that fulfills this interface.

```
1   type Database interface {
2       Query(query string) Result
3   }
4
5   type MockDatabase struct {
6       // Mock-specific fields and methods
7   }
8
9   func (m *MockDatabase) Query(query string) Result {
10      // Return a predefined result relevant for testing
11  }
```

Using this approach, the concurrent function can be tested with the MockDatabase instead of a real database, allowing the test to focus on the logic of the function rather than the database implementation.

Leveraging Channels for Mocking Asynchronous Behavior

Another powerful technique in Go for mocking concurrent dependencies involves the use of channels. Channels are at the heart of concurrency in Go, enabling goroutines to communicate with each other in a thread-safe manner. By using channels, one can mock asynchronous behaviors and concurrent interactions within the application.

For instance, if a piece of concurrent code is expected to receive data from an external service asynchronously via a channel, one can mock this behavior by sending predetermined data through a channel in the test environment.

```
func TestMyConcurrentFunction(t *testing.T) {
    mockDataChannel := make(chan DataType, 1)
    // Send mock data into the channel
    mockDataChannel <- MockData
    close(mockDataChannel)

    // Call the function being tested, providing the mock channel
    result := MyConcurrentFunction(mockDataChannel)

    // Assert that the function processes the mock data correctly
}
```

Using channels in this manner allows developers to simulate various concurrent scenarios, such as data arrival times and order, or the presence of errors, providing a robust mechanism for testing concurrent code.

Utilizing Third-Party Libraries for Advanced Mocking

While Go's standard library offers powerful tools for mocking, several third-party libraries can simplify and enhance the mocking of concurrent dependencies. Libraries such as "gomock" and "testify/mock" provide features such as automatic mock generation, more expressive assertion capabilities, and the ability to set expectations and verify interactions with the mocked objects. Leveraging these libraries can significantly reduce the boilerplate code required for mocking and make tests more expressive and easier to maintain.

```
1   // Example using testify/mock
2   mockDatabase := new(MockDatabase)
3   mockDatabase.On("Query", "SELECT * FROM table").Return(MockResult)
4
5   // Use mockDatabase in the test as if it were a real one
```

These libraries also encourage best practices in test design, promoting a clear separation between test setup, execution, and verification phases, which is particularly beneficial in the context of concurrent testing.

Mocking concurrent dependencies in Go is essential for creating deterministic and robust tests. By employing interfaces, channels, and third-party libraries, developers can effectively simulate complex and asynchronous behaviors, ensuring that concurrent code is both correct and performant. Leveraging these strategies not only aids in the testing process but also contributes to a more modular and testable codebase.

8.7 Integration Testing with Goroutines and Channels

Integration tests play a vital role in ensuring that the components of a concurrent application work together as expected. When it comes to Go, leveraging goroutines and channels is fundamental for the proper simulation of concurrent processes in integration tests. This section outlines the methodology for creating effective integration tests using these constructs.

Designing Integration Tests

When designing integration tests for concurrent Go applications, one must simulate the concurrent nature of production environments. This involves spawning multiple goroutines, potentially with varied duties, and coordinating their execution through channels.

```go
func TestIntegration(t *testing.T) {
    ch := make(chan string)
    go func() {
        ch <- "Data from concurrent operation"
    }()

    result := <-ch
    if result != "Data from concurrent operation" {
        t.Errorf("Expected result from channel was not received")
    }
}
```

The above example demonstrates a basic setup for an integration test involving goroutines and channels. The test simulates a concurrent operation by sending data through a channel from a goroutine, which is then received within the main test function.

Synchronization of Concurrent Processes

For more complex integration tests involving multiple concurrent processes, synchronization mechanisms provided by the "sync" package can be utilized, such as WaitGroups, to ensure that all concurrent operations have completed before assertions are made.

```go
func TestComplexIntegration(t *testing.T) {
    var wg sync.WaitGroup
    ch := make(chan string, 2) // Buffered channel
    wg.Add(2)

    go func() {
        defer wg.Done()
        ch <- "First piece of data"
    }()

    go func() {
        defer wg.Done()
        ch <- "Second piece of data"
    }()

    wg.Wait()
    close(ch)

    var results []string
    for result := range ch {
```

```
21        results = append(results, result)
22    }
23
24    if len(results) != 2 {
25        t.Errorf("Expected two results, got %v", len(results))
26    }
27 }
```

This example makes use of a buffered channel and a WaitGroup to orchestrate the completion of concurrent operations. The use of 'defer wg.Done()' ensures that the WaitGroup's counter is decremented as soon as the goroutine finishes its execution, signaling to the test that it can proceed with the assertion part.

Testing with Time-Sensitive Operations

In integration tests involving time-sensitive operations, such as timeouts or delays, the 'time' package offers tools for simulating or waiting for specific conditions.

```
1  func TestTimeSensitiveIntegration(t *testing.T) {
2      ch := make(chan bool)
3      go func() {
4          time.Sleep(100 * time.Millisecond)
5          ch <- true
6      }()
7
8      select {
9      case <-ch:
10         // Test succeeds
11     case <-time.After(150 * time.Millisecond):
12         t.Fatal("Test failed due to timeout")
13     }
14 }
```

The 'select' statement is used here to wait on multiple channel operations. The 'time.After' function creates a channel that sends the current time after a specified duration, effectively serving as a timeout mechanism for the test.

Effective integration testing of concurrent code in Go demands a deep understanding of goroutines, channels, and the synchronization mechanisms available in the "sync" and "time" packages. By combining these tools appropriately, developers can create comprehensive, accurate tests that closely mirror the conditions under which their concurrent applications will run in production.

8.8   Performance   Tuning: Profiling Concurrent Go Applications

In this section, we will discuss the practices for profiling concurrent Go applications to identify performance bottlenecks. Profiling is an essential step in tuning applications to achieve optimal performance. Go provides several built-in tools to facilitate this process.

Firstly, to profile Go applications, the pprof package is typically used. This package generates reports that help in understanding where an application spends its time or allocates its memory. The use of pprof in a concurrent application allows developers to pinpoint areas of the code that could be causing performance issues, such as goroutine bottlenecks or excessive memory usage.

To start a CPU profile, developers can use the following lines of code:

```
1  import _ "net/http/pprof"
2  import "net/http"
3
4  func main() {
5      go func() {
6          log.Println(http.ListenAndServe("localhost:6060", nil))
7      }()
8      // Your application logic here
9  }
```

By   navigating   to http://localhost:6060/debug/pprof/profile?seconds=30,   a CPU profile for the last 30 seconds of the application's execution can be downloaded. This file can then be analyzed using the go tool pprof command.

Memory profiling can be enabled in a similar fashion:

```
1  import _ "net/http/pprof"
2
3  // Same as above for starting the server
```

Then, access `http://localhost:6060/debug/pprof/heap` to get a snapshot of the current heap usage.

Analyzing the profiles requires understanding of the various visualizations and reports that pprof can generate. The text reports are useful for a quick overview, while the graph visualizations can provide deeper insights into the relationships between functions and goroutines.

To understand how memory is being allocated within the application, the following command can be used:

```
go tool pprof http://localhost:6060/debug/pprof/heap
```

Once inside the pprof tool, the text report can be generated using the `list` command followed by the function name. For a visual insight into memory allocation, the `web` command generates a graph that highlights the most significant memory users.

It's essential to profile applications under realistic load conditions to accurately identify performance bottlenecks. Therefore, consider using load testing tools to simulate real-world usage scenarios when profiling.

In addition to CPU and memory profiling, Go's pprof also supports block and goroutine profiling, which are particularly useful in concurrent applications. Block profiling helps identify where goroutines are being delayed, while goroutine profiling provides a count of existing goroutines, allowing developers to spot potential issues like goroutine leaks.

Finally, performance tuning is an iterative process. After making adjustments based on the profiling data, the application should be profiled again to determine the effect of the changes. By continuously refining the code in this manner, developers can significantly enhance the performance of their concurrent Go applications.

8.9   Testing for Deadlocks and Livelocks

Testing for deadlocks and livelocks in concurrent applications is a critical task to ensure that the system can handle multiple processes without stalling or entering into an infinite loop of non-productive activity. In Go, concurrency is a first-class citizen, but with great power comes the responsibility to ensure that goroutines interact smoothly, without causing the system to freeze or thrash.

To begin with, let's clarify what deadlocks and livelocks mean within the context of concurrent programming. A deadlock occurs when two or more processes hold resources and each process waits for the other to release their resources, leading to a standstill. On the other hand, a livelock is a situation where two or more processes continually change their states in response to each other without making any progress.

Detecting these issues involves a combination of static code analysis, testing techniques, and dynamic analysis tools. Static code analysis can be performed manually by inspecting the source code or automatically using tools designed to find potential deadlocks. However, due to the dynamic nature of concurrent execution, static analysis alone is often insufficient.

Dynamic analysis, especially through testing, becomes essential. The Go runtime provides several built-in facilities to aid in this process, most notably the -race flag and the sync package's Mutex functionalities for detecting race conditions, which can lead to deadlocks.

Implementing Deadlock Detection Tests

A practical approach to detecting deadlocks is to write tests that execute the concurrent code paths with the aim of triggering the deadlock condition, if it exists. This can be done by simulating the conditions under which a deadlock is likely to occur, and then observing if the test hangs. Here is a simple example using Go's testing framework:

```
1   package main
```

```
2
3   import (
4       "sync"
5       "testing"
6       "time"
7   )
8
9   func TestDeadlock(t *testing.T) {
10      var mutex1 sync.Mutex
11      var mutex2 sync.Mutex
12
13      go func() {
14          mutex1.Lock()
15          time.Sleep(time.Second) // Simulate work
16          mutex2.Lock()
17          mutex1.Unlock()
18          mutex2.Unlock()
19      }()
20
21      go func() {
22          mutex2.Lock()
23          time.Sleep(time.Second) // Simulate work
24          mutex1.Lock()
25          mutex2.Unlock()
26          mutex1.Unlock()
27      }()
28
29      time.Sleep(3 * time.Second) // Wait enough time for the deadlock to manifest
30  }
```

In this example, two goroutines attempt to acquire two mutexes in opposite orders. If left unchecked, this scenario results in a classic deadlock. The test doesn't assert anything but relies on the deadlock detector built into the Go runtime, which will automatically panic if a deadlock is detected when the program is run with the -race flag.

Detecting Livelocks

Testing for livelocks follows a similar methodology but focuses on ensuring that the system makes progress rather than getting stuck in a state of continuous activity. Monitoring the state of the application to ensure continuous progression can achieve this. Here's a conceptual guideline:

1. Identify critical sections of the code where livelocks are suspected.

231

2. Implement monitoring at these points to track the application's state over time.

3. Develop tests that stress the system under conditions prone to triggering livelocks.

4. Analyze the state monitoring logs to verify that progress is continually made.

Testing for deadlocks and livelocks is an ongoing process that benefits significantly from comprehensive test coverage and continuous integration practices. By integrating these tests into the CI pipeline, potential issues can be caught early in the development cycle, significantly reducing the risk of concurrency-related bugs making it into production.

8.10   Best Practices for Testable Concurrent Design

In this section, we will discuss several methodologies that facilitate the creation of concurrent Go applications that are easier to test, debug, and maintain. Adhering to these practices can significantly improve the reliability and performance of concurrent code.

Isolation of Concurrency Mechanisms: The first principle in designing testable concurrent applications is the isolation of concurrency mechanisms from business logic.   This implies separating the code responsible for managing threads, goroutines, and synchronization primitives from the code executing the actual application logic.

- For instance, if a function is responsible for fetching data concurrently from multiple sources, it should delegate the data fetching logic to individual goroutines without embedding the concurrency logic within the data processing itself.

```
1   func fetchDataConcurrently(urls []string) []*Result {
2       var wg sync.WaitGroup
3       results := make([]*Result, len(urls))
4       for i, url := range urls {
5           wg.Add(1)
6           go func(i int, url string) {
7               defer wg.Done()
8               results[i] = fetchData(url)
9           }(i, url)
10      }
11      wg.Wait()
12      return results
13  }
```

This code snippet illustrates how concurrency is managed separately from the fetchData function, which represents the core logic.

- Design interfaces that abstract out concurrency mechanisms, allowing the underlying implementation to use goroutines, channels, or other concurrency primitives without exposing these details to the consuming code.

Use of Channels for Communication: Channels in Go provide a powerful way to communicate between goroutines safely. When designing concurrent applications, channels should be used for passing data and control signals between goroutines to avoid shared memory issues and race conditions.

- Channels can be used to implement safe termination of goroutines by signaling them to stop work and exit. This is a cleaner approach compared to using shared variables or other synchronization primitives.

```
1   func worker(done chan bool) {
2       fmt.Println("Working...")
3       time.Sleep(time.Second)
4       fmt.Println("Done")
5
6       // Signal that work is finished.
7       done <- true
8   }
9
10  func main() {
11      done := make(chan bool, 1)
```

```
12      go worker(done)
13
14      // Wait for the worker to send a signal.
15      <-done
16    }
```

In the example above, a done channel is used to signal the completion of a goroutine's execution, demonstrating the use of channels for communication and control between goroutines.

Leveraging Race Detectors and Locks: Go provides a built-in race detector that can be invoked with the -race flag during testing to detect race conditions in concurrent code. Additionally, using mutexes (mutual exclusion locks) can help protect shared resources from concurrent access, thus preventing race conditions.

- Regularly run the race detector during development and testing to catch and fix race conditions early in the development cycle.

- Use mutexes to synchronize access to shared variables or resources among multiple goroutines. However, avoid overusing locks as they can lead to deadlocks and reduce the performance of the application.

Avoiding Global State: Another best practice for concurrent design is to avoid global state. Global variables and shared state can introduce hidden dependencies among goroutines, leading to subtle bugs and race conditions.

- If shared state is necessary, encapsulate it within a struct and use methods with proper synchronization mechanisms to safely access or modify it.

- Favor passing data explicitly between goroutines through parameters or channels rather than relying on shared global state.

Testing Concurrency with Integration and End-to-End Tests: While unit tests are essential for testing individual components in isolation, concurrency issues often manifest at the integration or application level. Therefore, it's crucial to write comprehensive integration and end-to-end tests that simulate real-world usage of the concurrent application.

- Use Go's testing package and third-party tools to simulate concurrent operations and interactions in tests.

- Test for edge cases and scenarios that are likely to trigger race conditions or deadlocks, such as high levels of concurrency or specific timing conditions.

By following these best practices, developers can create Go applications that leverage concurrency effectively while remaining maintainable, reliable, and easy to test.

8.11 Continuous Integration for Concurrent Applications

Continuous Integration (CI) stands as a pivotal practice in the realm of software development, particularly accentuated in the context of concurrent applications. The nature of concurrency introduces nuanced challenges that demand a systemic and automated approach to ensure code quality and functionality. CI systems automate the building, testing, and deployment processes, providing immediate feedback on the codebase's health. This section sheds light on how to seamlessly integrate CI into the workflow of developing concurrent applications in Go, leveraging its testing tools and emphasizing practices that mitigate common concurrency pitfalls.

The integration of CI into a concurrent Go application involves several key steps, starting with the selection of a CI tool. Popular options include Jenkins, Travis CI, GitHub Actions, and CircleCI. Each offers a unique set of features and integrations, but the foundational setup for a Go project remains relatively consistent. Below is an outline of essential practices for configuring a CI pipeline for Go applications:

- Initializing the CI environment with the necessary version of Go.

- Installing dependencies needed for the build and test phases.

- Running unit tests, including those designed for concurrent functions, using Go's built-in testing suite.

- Employing race detection during testing to uncover potential data races in concurrent operations.

- Benchmarking concurrent code to ensure performance criteria are met.

- Automating the deployment of the application upon successful integration and testing phases.

Configuring the pipeline to execute the unit tests for concurrent code is of paramount importance. Tests for concurrent functions should be designed to run with the '-race' flag to enable the race detector. Here is an example of how to configure a job in a CI tool to run Go tests with race detection:

```
go test -v ./... -race
```

The '-v' flag is included for verbose output, and './...' specifies that tests should be run recursively in all packages of the project. The '-race' flag activates the race detector, a crucial tool in identifying race conditions.

Upon the detection of a race condition or a failing test, the CI pipeline should halt, and feedback should be provided. This instant notification allows developers to address concurrency issues promptly, well before the code is merged into the main branch. Configuring automated notifications, either through email, Slack, or another communication platform integrated with the chosen CI tool, facilitates this rapid response mechanism.

In addition to automated testing, setting up a benchmarking step in the CI pipeline highlights any regressions in the performance of concurrent operations. This can be achieved via the Go testing tool, as displayed in the given example:

```
1   go test -bench=.
```

The '-bench=.' flag instructs Go to run benchmarks across the project. Monitoring these results over time can provide critical insights into the impact of changes on performance, enabling developers to make informed optimization choices.

It is also worthwhile to incorporate static analysis tools into the CI pipeline to scrutinize code quality and detect potential issues, such as deadlocks or ineffective synchronization practices, that could degrade the concurrency model's efficiency.

Finally, ensuring the CI pipeline is integrated into the version control system allows for automated triggering of builds and tests upon each commit or pull request. This practice enforces a culture of regular, incremental improvements and testing, laying the groundwork for robust and reliable concurrent Go applications.

The integration of Continuous Integration practices into the development workflow of concurrent Go applications advances both the software's quality and the team's productivity. By automating build, test, and deployment processes, CI helps uncover and address concurrency-related issues early, maintains performance standards, and supports a sustainable development lifecycle.

8.12   Tools and Libraries for Testing Concurrent Code

Testing concurrent code in Go requires a nuanced approach, as the inherent nondeterminism of concurrent execution can lead to subtle bugs that are difficult to reproduce and diagnose. Fortunately, a diverse set of tools and libraries are available within the Go ecosystem to aid in this process. This section focuses on a selection of these tools and libraries, elucidating their unique features and demonstrating how they can be applied to improve the reliability and performance of concurrent Go code.

The Go Race Detector

A pivotal tool provided by the Go toolchain is the Race Detector. This tool is instrumental in identifying race conditions within concurrent code segments. To use the Race Detector, one must merely pass the -race flag to the go test command as follows:

```
1  go test -race ./...
```

The above command triggers the execution of unit tests across the entire module, with the Race Detector actively analyzing memory accesses by concurrent goroutines to identify potential data races.

Gomega and Ginkgo

For more expressive testing, the combination of Gomega and Ginkgo offers a robust solution. Ginkgo is a testing framework designed specifically for Go, which, when used in conjunction with Gomega—a matcher/assertion library—facilitates behavior-driven development (BDD) for Go applications, including those that are concurrent in nature. The following example illustrates how to use these libraries to test concurrent code:

```
1   package mypackage
2
3   import (
4       . "github.com/onsi/ginkgo"
5       . "github.com/onsi/gomega"
6   )
7
8   var _ = Describe("ConcurrentFunction", func() {
9       It("executes without error", func() {
10          err := ConcurrentFunction()
11          Expect(err).ToNot(HaveOccurred())
12      })
13  })
```

This example showcases how Ginkgo's BDD style can make tests more readable and how Gomega's assertions simplify the process of verifying the behavior of concurrent functions.

GoConvey

Another powerful tool in the arsenal for testing concurrent Go code is GoConvey. This tool extends Go's native testing package to offer a more expressive, browser-based user interface for writing and running tests. It supports automatic re-running of tests upon source code changes, making it particularly useful for iterative development processes. An example of using GoConvey for testing concurrent operations is as follows:

```
 1  package mypackage
 2
 3  import (
 4      . "github.com/smartystreets/goconvey/convey"
 5      "testing"
 6  )
 7
 8  func TestConcurrentFunction(t *testing.T) {
 9      Convey("Given a running concurrent function", t, func() {
10          Convey("It should execute without error", func() {
11              err := ConcurrentFunction()
12              So(err, ShouldBeNil)
13          })
14      })
15  }
```

This example demonstrates GoConvey's expressive syntax, which aids in describing tests in a more human-readable format.

benchstat

When it comes to benchmarking concurrent code, benchstat is an invaluable tool. It provides a simple way to compare benchmark results, helping to identify performance regressions or improvements. After generating benchmark data using the go test -bench command, benchstat can be used to statistically analyze the results for significant changes as follows:

```
 1  benchstat old.txt new.txt
```

Here, old.txt and new.txt represent files containing benchmark results from different code versions, allowing developers to quantitatively assess the impact of code changes on performance.

Each of these tools and libraries plays a distinct role in the testing and benchmarking of concurrent Go code. By integrating them into the development workflow, developers can significantly enhance the correctness and performance of their concurrent applications.

Chapter 9

Patterns for Concurrent Programming

Design patterns provide a reusable solution to common problems in software design, and concurrent programming in Go is no exception. This chapter introduces and explores a variety of concurrency patterns that are particularly effective in Go, such as the worker pool, pipeline, and fan-in/fan-out patterns. Each pattern is detailed with practical examples, showcasing how they can simplify the development of complex concurrent applications by structuring them in a more manageable, scalable, and efficient manner. Understanding these patterns enables developers to leverage Go's concurrency model to its fullest, resulting in software that is both robust and performant.

9.1 Introduction to Concurrent Design Patterns

In this section, we will discuss the fundamental principles of concurrent design patterns within the context of the Go programming language. Design patterns are essentially templates devised to solve common problems in software design. When applied to concurrent programming, these patterns provide a structured approach to designing, developing, and deploying applications that efficiently manage and execute multiple tasks simultaneously.

The core of Go's approach to concurrency revolves around Goroutines and Channels. Goroutines are functions or methods that run concurrently with other functions or methods. Channels, on the other hand, are conduits that allow the exchange of values between Goroutines. The synergy between Goroutines and Channels underpins the various concurrent design patterns we will explore in this chapter.

Let's start with the concurrency primitives provided by Go:

- Goroutines: Lightweight threads managed by the Go runtime. They are launched by prefixing a function call with the go keyword. The scheduling of these Goroutines is handled by the Go runtime, making the creation and management of concurrent tasks straightforward and efficient.

```
1   go func() {
2       fmt.Println("Hello from a Goroutine")
3   }()
```

- Channels: Typed conduits that enable the safe exchange of data between Goroutines, effectively allowing them to synchronize their execution without explicit locks or condition variables. Channels can be buffered or unbuffered, influencing the behavior and performance of the concurrent operations they coordinate.

```
1   messages := make(chan string)
2
3   go func() { messages <- "ping" }()
4
5   msg := <-messages
6   fmt.Println(msg)
```

    ping

These primitives are the building blocks of concurrent programming in Go and form the foundation upon which the concurrent design patterns are constructed.

Design patterns in concurrent programming serve multiple purposes:

- They provide a high-level language for discussing program design.

- They facilitate the reuse of successful architectural solutions.

- They offer solutions that boost the performance and scalability of applications.

- They enable programmers to develop non-trivial concurrent applications with less effort and error.

In this chapter, we will delve into specific patterns tailored for concurrency, including the worker pool pattern, which enables efficient processing of tasks by a pool of worker Goroutines; the pipeline pattern, which chains processing steps executed in sequence; and the fan-in and fan-out patterns, which are useful for distributing tasks among workers and aggregating results, respectively. Additionally, patterns such as publish/subscribe and future/promise provide mechanisms for non-blocking data exchange and asynchronous task execution.

Through the exploration of these patterns and their practical examples, developers will gain an understanding of how to structure their concurrent applications effectively. This knowledge empowers developers to harness the concurrency features of Go, crafting applications that are scalable, efficient, and maintainable.

9.2 The Worker Pool Pattern

The worker pool pattern is a structural concurrency design pattern aimed at enhancing the efficiency and throughput of concurrent applications. It involves creating a finite number of worker goroutines to perform multiple tasks in parallel. This pattern is particularly useful when there's a large set of tasks to be executed, but the system resources are limited, necessitating a control over the number of concurrent operations.

To implement the worker pool pattern in Go, one typically utilizes channels and goroutines. Channels serve as conduits for tasks and results, while goroutines act as the workers that execute the tasks. The fundamental steps involved in this pattern include initiating a pool of worker goroutines, distributing tasks among them through channels, and collecting the results.

Below is a step-by-step implementation of the worker-pool pattern in Go:

```
 1  package main
 2
 3  import (
 4      "fmt"
 5      "sync"
 6      "time"
 7  )
 8
 9  type Job struct {
10      id int
11      randomno int
12  }
13
14  type Result struct {
15      job Job
16      sumofdigits int
17  }
18
19  var jobs = make(chan Job, 10)
20  var results = make(chan Result, 10)
21
22  func digits(number int) int {
23      sum := 0
24      no := number
25      for no != 0 {
26          digit := no % 10
27          sum += digit
28          no /= 10
29      }
30      time.Sleep(2 * time.Second)
31      return sum
32  }
33
34  func worker(wg *sync.WaitGroup) {
35      for job := range jobs{
36          output := Result{job, digits(job.randomno)}
37          results <- output
```

```
38        }
39        wg.Done()
40   }
41
42   func createWorkerPool(noOfWorkers int) {
43        var wg sync.WaitGroup
44        for i := 0; i < noOfWorkers; i++ {
45             wg.Add(1)
46             go worker(&wg)
47        }
48        wg.Wait()
49        close(results)
50   }
51
52   func allocate(noOfJobs int) {
53        for i := 0; i < noOfJobs; i++ {
54             randomno := rand.Intn(999)
55             job := Job{i, randomno}
56             jobs <- job
57        }
58        close(jobs)
59   }
60
61   func result(done chan bool) {
62        for result := range results {
63             fmt.Printf("Job id %d, input random no %d , sum of digits %d\n", result.
                    job.id, result.job.randomno, result.sumofdigits)
64        }
65        done <- true
66   }
67
68   func main() {
69        startTime := time.Now()
70        noOfJobs := 100
71        go allocate(noOfJobs)
72        done := make(chan bool)
73        go result(done)
74        noOfWorkers := 10
75        createWorkerPool(noOfWorkers)
76        <-done
77        endTime := time.Now()
78        diff := endTime.Sub(startTime)
79        fmt.Println("total time taken ", diff.Seconds(), "seconds")
80   }
```

This code snippet demonstrates a basic worker pool in Go. The Job struct contains information about each task, and the Result struct captures the output of each job completed by the workers. The digits function simulates a task that calculates the sum of the digits of a given number, mimicking a CPU-bound operation.

The worker function is a goroutine that continuously receives jobs from the jobs channel, performs the task, and sends the results to the results channel. The createWorkerPool function launches a specified number of workers, ensuring that the system utilizes a fixed number of goroutines to execute the tasks concurrently. The allocate function distributes jobs among the workers by sending jobs to the jobs channel. Finally, the result function collects and prints the results of completed jobs.

The worker pool pattern efficiently distributes tasks among a fixed set of workers, allowing for controlled concurrency that can lead to improved throughput and performance of applications. It shows how Go's channels and goroutines can be leveraged to implement sophisticated concurrency patterns with relative ease.

9.3   The Pipeline Pattern

The Pipeline pattern is a structural design pattern that provides a methodology for decomposing a task into a series of sequential processing stages. Each stage in the pipeline is responsible for a specific aspect of the task and passes its output to the next stage in the sequence. This is particularly powerful in Go due to its first-class support for concurrency with goroutines and channels.

Implementing the Pipeline pattern in Go involves creating a series of functions where each function launches a goroutine for processing and communicates via channels. To illustrate, consider a scenario where data needs to be processed through three stages: preprocessing, processing, and postprocessing.

First, define the functions to represent each stage of the pipeline:

```
1   func preprocess(in <-chan int) <-chan int {
2       out := make(chan int)
3       go func() {
4           for n := range in {
5               out <- n * 2 // Example operation
6           }
7           close(out)
8       }()
9       return out
10  }
11
```

```
12   func process(in <-chan int) <-chan int {
13       out := make(chan int)
14       go func() {
15           for n := range in {
16               out <- n + 3 // Example operation
17           }
18           close(out)
19       }()
20       return out
21   }
22
23   func postprocess(in <-chan int) <-chan int {
24       out := make(chan int)
25       go func() {
26           for n := range in {
27               out <- n - 1 // Example operation
28           }
29           close(out)
30       }()
31       return out
32   }
```

To assemble these stages into a pipeline, input is fed into the first stage, and the output of one stage is connected to the input of the next:

```
1    func main() {
2        // Source data.
3        in := make(chan int)
4
5        // Initialize the pipeline.
6        pp := preprocess(in)
7        p := process(pp)
8        po := postprocess(p)
9
10       // Send data into the pipeline.
11       go func() {
12           for i := 0; i <= 10; i++ {
13               in <- i
14           }
15           close(in)
16       }()
17
18       // Receive and print the output of the pipeline.
19       for n := range po {
20           fmt.Println(n)
21       }
22   }
```

The output of the program shows the processed data at each stage of the pipeline:

2
5
8
11
14
17
20
23
26
29

This implementation demonstrates the primary advantages of the Pipeline pattern: easy to understand and debug, can be scaled by distributing stages across multiple goroutines or even different machines, and each stage can be tested independently. Moreover, due to the blocking nature of Go channels, the pipeline provides a natural back-pressure mechanism, preventing any stage from being overwhelmed by too much input.

Care must be taken to ensure that the pipeline is properly terminated, generally by closing the input channel and ensuring that all goroutines exit cleanly, to avoid leaking resources.

By affording a structured approach to concurrent programming, the Pipeline pattern in Go enables the development of efficient, scalable, and maintainable applications.

9.4   The Fan-in and Fan-out Patterns

In this section, we will discuss the Fan-in and Fan-out patterns, which are pivotal in managing tasks that can be executed in parallel, thereby maximizing throughput and efficiency in a concurrent Go application. These patterns, when rightly applied, streamline the process of distributing workload across multiple goroutines (Fan-out) and then consolidating the results through a single channel (Fan-in).

Fan-out Pattern

The Fan-out pattern involves starting multiple goroutines to handle tasks concurrently. This pattern is particularly useful when tasks are independent of each other and can be performed in parallel without waiting for one another. The essence of the Fan-out pattern is to maximize CPU utilization by distributing tasks across available CPU cores.

Consider a scenario where we need to process a large number of requests. Instead of processing these requests sequentially, we can use the Fan-out pattern to handle multiple requests in parallel. Here is a simple example demonstrating the Fan-out pattern:

```go
package main

import (
    "fmt"
    "sync"
    "time"
)

func worker(id int, jobs <-chan int, results chan<- int) {
    for j := range jobs {
        fmt.Println("worker", id, "started job", j)
        time.Sleep(time.Second)
        fmt.Println("worker", id, "finished job", j)
        results <- j * 2
    }
}

func main() {
    jobs := make(chan int, 100)
    results := make(chan int, 100)

    for w := 1; w <= 3; w++ {
        go worker(w, jobs, results)
    }

    for j := 1; j <= 9; j++ {
        jobs <- j
    }
    close(jobs)

    for a := 1; a <= 9; a++ {
```

```
32          <-results
33      }
34  }
```

In the above example, we create three worker goroutines that concurrently process elements from the jobs channel. The results of the computation are then sent to the results channel. This demonstrates the Fan-out pattern, where multiple tasks are being handled concurrently by different workers.

Fan-in Pattern

Conversely, the Fan-in pattern is used to combine multiple results into a single channel. This is especially useful when you want to aggregate results from multiple concurrent operations. The Fan-in pattern can significantly simplify the synchronization of concurrent tasks as they complete.

Here's an example that demonstrates how to implement the Fan-in pattern:

```
1   package main
2
3   import (
4       "fmt"
5       "sync"
6   )
7
8   func merge(cs ...<-chan int) <-chan int {
9       var wg sync.WaitGroup
10      out := make(chan int)
11
12      output := func(c <-chan int) {
13          for n := range c {
14              out <- n
15          }
16          wg.Done()
17      }
18      wg.Add(len(cs))
19      for _, c := range cs {
20          go output(c)
21      }
22
```

```
23    go func() {
24        wg.Wait()
25        close(out)
26    }()
27    return out
28  }
```

In this implementation, multiple channels are merged into a single output channel. The merge function creates a goroutine for each input channel that forwards the contents to the output channel. Once all input channels are closed, and their contents have been forwarded, the output channel is closed. This exemplifies the Fan-in pattern, showcasing how results from different concurrent processes can be aggregated and synchronized efficiently.

These two patterns, Fan-in and Fan-out, are fundamental in developing efficient and scalable concurrent programs in Go. By understanding and implementing these patterns, developers can fully leverage Go's concurrency model to build high-performance applications.

9.5 The Publish/Subscribe Pattern

The Publish/Subscribe pattern, often abbreviated as Pub/Sub, is a messaging paradigm where senders of messages, known as publishers, do not program the messages to be sent directly to specific receivers, or subscribers. Instead, published messages are characterized into classes without knowledge of which subscribers, if any, there might be. Similarly, subscribers express interest in one or more classes and only receive messages that are of interest, without knowledge of which publishers, if any, there are. This decoupling of publishers and subscribers helps in the development of scalable and manageable code, especially in the context of concurrent programming in Go.

In Go, the Pub/Sub pattern can be effectively implemented using goroutines and channels. Channels act as a conduit for messages between publishers and subscribers, whereas goroutines handle the concurrent execution of Pub/Sub operations.

To demonstrate the Pub/Sub pattern in Go, let's consider a simple scenario where we have a system that publishes news articles on various topics, and subscribers can subscribe to topics of interest to receive relevant news articles.

```go
package main

import (
    "fmt"
    "sync"
)

type Article struct {
    Title string
    Content string
    Topic string
}

type PubSub struct {
    mu sync.RWMutex
    subscribers map[string][]chan Article
}

func NewPubSub() *PubSub {
    return &PubSub{
        subscribers: make(map[string][]chan Article),
    }
}

func (ps *PubSub) Subscribe(topic string) <-chan Article {
    ps.mu.Lock()
    defer ps.mu.Unlock()

    ch := make(chan Article, 1) // Create a new channel for the subscriber
    ps.subscribers[topic] = append(ps.subscribers[topic], ch)

    return ch
}

func (ps *PubSub) Publish(article Article) {
    ps.mu.RLock()
    defer ps.mu.RUnlock()

    subscribers, exists := ps.subscribers[article.Topic]
    if !exists {
        return // No subscribers for the topic
    }

    // Send the article to all subscribers of the topic
    for _, ch := range subscribers {
        ch <- article
    }
}

func main() {
```

```
51    ps := NewPubSub()
52
53    // Subscribe to "sports" topic
54    sportsChannel := ps.Subscribe("sports")
55    go func() {
56        for article := range sportsChannel {
57            fmt.Printf("Received article on sports: %s\n", article.Title)
58        }
59    }()
60
61    // Publish an article on "sports"
62    ps.Publish(Article{Title: "Local Team Wins!", Content: "Details about the
          game...", Topic: "sports"})
63  }
```

In this implementation, the PubSub struct functions as the central component managing subscriptions and publishing articles. The Subscribe method allows subscribers to register interest in a specific topic and returns a channel through which they receive published articles. The Publish method is used by publishers to send articles to interested subscribers based on the article's topic.

This pattern fosters a clean separation of concerns between components that produce data (publishers) and those that consume it (subscribers). It's particularly useful in applications that require a high degree of decoupling and scalability. The use of channels in Go's implementation of this pattern naturally fits the concurrency model, making the Pub/Sub pattern a powerful and efficient choice for concurrent programming in Go.

9.6 The Future and Promise Pattern

The Future and Promise pattern in concurrent programming, particularly within the context of Go, serves as a powerful mechanism for synchronizing asynchronous operations and managing the results of these operations once they complete. This pattern decomposes tasks into manageable, isolated computational units that work independently, enhancing the scalability and maintainability of complex software systems.

At the heart of the Future and Promise pattern lies the abstraction of a 'future': a proxy for a result that is initially unknown but will become available at some point. The 'promise', on the other hand, acts as a writable, single assignment container which sets the value of the future. When a promise is fulfilled, any computations waiting on the future can proceed with the now available result.

To implement the Future and Promise pattern in Go, one can leverage channels and goroutines, enabling a seamless orchestration of asynchronous tasks. Consider the following example:

```go
package main

import (
    "fmt"
    "time"
)

// A function to simulate a task that returns a result in the future.
func performTask() <-chan int {
    result := make(chan int)
    go func() {
        // Simulate a task taking 3 seconds.
        time.Sleep(3 * time.Second)
        result <- 42 // Sending the result back through the channel.
    }()
    return result
}

func main() {
    future := performTask()
    fmt.Println("Task initiated. Waiting for the result...")

    result := <-future // Waiting and receiving the result.
    fmt.Printf("Received result: %d\n", result)
}
```

In this example, the performTask function launches a goroutine that simulates processing by sleeping for 3 seconds, then sends a value (42) through a channel. This channel is returned as a 'future' that will eventually hold the result of the asynchronous operation. The main function initiates the task and immediately proceeds to wait for the result, effectively demonstrating the Future and Promise pattern.

The output of this program will be:

```
Task initiated. Waiting for the result...
```

```
Received result: 42
```

By using this pattern, developers can manage the complexities associated with asynchronous computations by focusing on the coordination and synchronization of these tasks, rather than getting entangled in the intricacies of their implementation details.

Furthermore, the Future and Promise pattern promotes a clear separation of concerns, thereby significantly improving code readability and maintainability. It enables developers to structure their programs in a way that parallellizable tasks can be executed concurrently, without the need for intricate error handling and synchronization mechanisms typically associated with concurrent programming.

In summary, leveraging the Future and Promise pattern in Go applications allows for efficient task orchestration, error handling, and result management in asynchronous programming contexts, bringing forth scalable and robust software solutions.

9.7 The Singleton Pattern in a Concurrent World

The Singleton pattern is a software design pattern that ensures a class has only one instance and provides a global point of access to it. While the concept is straightforward in a single-threaded environment, applying the Singleton pattern in a concurrent world, such as in Go, requires careful consideration to maintain thread safety and performance.

Understanding the Singleton Pattern

At its core, the Singleton pattern intends to control object creation by preventing direct instantiation from outside the class and allowing only one instance to be created. This is particularly useful for accessing shared resources or services throughout an application, such as a database connection pool or a configuration manager.

Challenges in a Concurrent Context

However, in a concurrent environment, multiple threads or goroutines may attempt to create the instance simultaneously, leading to potential race conditions. It is crucial to ensure that the class is thread-safe so that only one instance is ever created, even when multiple threads are involved.

Implementing Singleton Safely in Go

To implement a thread-safe Singleton in Go, one can use the 'sync' package, which provides synchronization primitives such as mutexes. A common approach is to use a combination of the 'sync.Once' type and a private variable that holds the instance. 'sync.Once' ensures that a function is executed only once, regardless of how many times it is called, making it ideal for initializing the Singleton instance.

```
import (
    "sync"
)

type singleton struct {}

var instance *singleton
var once sync.Once

func GetInstance() *singleton {
    once.Do(func() {
        instance = &singleton{}
    })
    return instance
}
```

This code snippet defines a 'singleton' struct and a private variable 'instance' to hold the Singleton instance. The 'GetInstance' function uses 'once.Do' to ensure that the 'instance' is initialized only once, thus adhering to the Singleton pattern's requirement in a thread-safe manner.

Drawbacks and Considerations

While the Singleton pattern can be incredibly useful, it is not without its drawbacks, especially in a concurrent programming context. One significant concern is the potential for hidden dependencies, as global access to the Singleton instance can make it difficult to track which parts of an application depend on it. Furthermore, extensively using the Singleton pattern may lead to issues with code testability and flexibility due to the tight coupling it introduces.

Alternatives to Singleton

Given these considerations, developers should carefully assess whether the Singleton pattern is the right choice for their application. Alternatives such as dependency injection or using package-level variables in Go may provide similar benefits without some of the drawbacks associated with Singletons.

To summarize, implementing the Singleton pattern in a concurrent world such as Go's requires a careful approach to ensure thread safety and performance. While the pattern can provide significant advantages, it is essential to consider its implications and explore alternatives when appropriate. By doing so, developers can make informed decisions that lead to cleaner, more maintainable, and efficient concurrent applications.

9.8 Error Handling in Concurrent Patterns

Error handling in concurrent programming models, particularly with Go, demands a structured and deliberate approach. Given the nature of concurrent operations - where multiple threads or goroutines are executing in parallel - the traditional methods of error handling such as relying on exception propagation become impractical. This section will discuss effective strategies for managing errors in concurrent patterns, illustrating how these can be implemented in Go to build robust and fault-tolerant systems.

Go does not use exceptions; instead, it follows a simple yet powerful error handling model where errors are returned as normal values. This model fits well with Go's philosophy of simplicity and clarity, but it presents unique challenges in a concurrent context. These challenges stem primarily from the need to collect and handle errors from multiple concurrent operations.

One fundamental strategy is the use of error channels. An error channel is a Go channel through which goroutines can send error values back to a central point of error handling. This allows a parent goroutine to spawn multiple worker goroutines and efficiently monitor them for errors.

```
func worker(input <-chan Data, output chan<- Result, errors chan<- error) {
    for data := range input {
        result, err := doWork(data)
        if err != nil {
            errors <- err
            return
        }
        output <- result
    }
}
```

In the example above, the worker function takes an input channel for data, an output channel for results, and an errors channel for communicating any encountered errors back to the caller. The doWork function represents any task that might fail, returning a result or an error.

The main routine that manages these workers must then be prepared to handle incoming errors on the error channel. This can be achieved through select statements that listen on multiple channels, including the error channel.

```
errors := make(chan error, numWorkers)
// Initialization of workers and other channels omitted for brevity

for {
    select {
    case err := <-errors:
        log.Printf("Error encountered: %v", err)
        // Handle error, possibly terminating all workers gracefully
        return
    case result := <-results:
        // Process result
    // Additional cases for other channels, like a done channel
```

```
13        }
14    }
```

By using a `select` statement, the main routine can react to errors as they happen, logging them, recovering if possible, or terminating operations gracefully if necessary. It is crucial, however, to ensure that the error channels are appropriately buffered or monitored to prevent worker goroutines from being blocked when sending errors, potentially leading to deadlocks.

Apart from error channels, it's also possible to aggregate errors from multiple goroutines, allowing the parent routine to collect and process errors after all workers have completed. This method is particularly useful when it's acceptable to wait for all operations to conclude before handling errors.

```
1    var wg sync.WaitGroup
2    for _, task := range tasks {
3        wg.Add(1)
4        go func(task Task) {
5            defer wg.Done()
6            if err := task.Do(); err != nil {
7                // Aggregate errors
8            }
9        }(task)
10   }
11   wg.Wait()
12   // Process any aggregated errors here
```

In this approach, a `sync.WaitGroup` is used to wait for all goroutines to finish, and errors can be aggregated in a thread-safe manner, using mechanisms such as mutexes or concurrent-safe data structures provided by Go's standard library.

Error handling in concurrent patterns requires attention to the intricacies of parallel execution flows and the potential for simultaneous error conditions. By leveraging Go's channels, select statements, and synchronization primitives, it is possible to implement robust error handling mechanisms that contribute to the overall resilience and reliability of concurrent applications.

9.9   Load Balancing with Go Channels

Load balancing is a critical concept in concurrent programming, particularly for applications that handle a large number of tasks concurrently. In Go, channels provide an excellent mechanism for distributing work among multiple goroutines in a way that balances the load effectively. This section will explain the principles of load balancing in the context of Go concurrency and demonstrate how to implement a load balancer using channels.

Load balancing involves distributing work among several workers (goroutines, in Go's case) so that no single worker is overwhelmed by too many tasks, ensuring that all tasks are completed efficiently. The main goal is to maximize resource utilization and minimize task completion time. Go's channels are ideal for this purpose as they provide a way to both distribute tasks and collect results in a thread-safe manner.

Implementing a load balancer with Go channels typically involves the following components:

- A dispatcher that sends tasks to multiple worker goroutines through input channels.

- Worker goroutines that process tasks and return results.

- An aggregator that collects results from worker goroutines.

Let us consider a basic example where we have a fixed number of workers, and we want to distribute tasks among them evenly.

```
1   package main
2
3   import (
4       "fmt"
5       "time"
6   )
7
8   func worker(id int, tasks <-chan int, results chan<- int) {
9       for t := range tasks {
10          fmt.Printf("Worker %d started task %d\n", id, t)
11          time.Sleep(time.Second) // Simulate time-consuming task
12          fmt.Printf("Worker %d finished task %d\n", id, t)
```

```
13          results <- t * 2 // Send back results
14      }
15  }
16
17  func main() {
18      tasks := make(chan int, 100)
19      results := make(chan int, 100)
20
21      // Start 5 workers.
22      for w := 1; w <= 5; w++ {
23          go worker(w, tasks, results)
24      }
25
26      // Send 10 tasks.
27      for t := 1; t <= 10; t++ {
28          tasks <- t
29      }
30      close(tasks) // No more tasks to send.
31
32      // Collect all results.
33      for a := 1; a <= 10; a++ {
34          <-results
35      }
36  }
```

In this example, a dispatcher (the main function) sends tasks to worker goroutines through the tasks channel. Each worker goroutine processes tasks sent via the tasks channel and sends the results back through the results channel. Once a worker finishes processing a task, it reads the next task from the tasks channel, effectively balancing the load across workers.

Output when running the program might look like this:

```
Worker 1 started task 1
Worker 2 started task 2
Worker 3 started task 3
Worker 4 started task 4
Worker 5 started task 5
Worker 1 finished task 1
Worker 1 started task 6
Worker 2 finished task 2
Worker 2 started task 7
...
```

This output demonstrates that tasks are distributed among the available workers. As soon as a worker is free, it picks up the next task from the tasks channel, ensuring that all workers are utilized effectively.

To further enhance the load balancing mechanism, one could implement dynamic worker spawning based on the workload or use a priority queue to manage tasks based on their urgency or complexity. The flexibility of Go channels makes it straightforward to adapt the load balancing strategy according to specific requirements.

Implementing a load balancer using Go channels is a powerful pattern for achieving efficient task distribution among goroutines. By leveraging Go's concurrency primitives, developers can create robust applications capable of handling high workloads with optimal resource utilization.

9.10 Pattern: Managing   State   with Goroutines

Managing state in concurrent applications can introduce complexity and lead to issues such as race conditions if not handled correctly. Go, with its goroutines and channels, offers a pattern that simplifies state management in concurrent environments.   This section discusses how to manage state using goroutines, ensuring safe access to shared data by serializing its access through Go channels.

The core idea behind this pattern is to encapsulate the state within a single goroutine and allow other goroutines to read or modify this state only by sending messages to this goroutine. This approach, often referred to as the "actor model", ensures that only one goroutine manipulates the state at any given time, thus preventing race conditions.

Implementing State Management with Goroutines

The implementation involves creating a struct to represent the state, along with a set of operations (functions) that can be performed on the state. A dedicated goroutine, henceforth called the state manager, runs an infinite loop, processing requests to access or modify the state. This is achieved by defining a set of request and response types as

well as a mechanism for other goroutines to send these requests to
the state manager goroutine and receive responses.

```go
type state struct {
    // Define the state variables
    counter int
}

type incrementRequest struct {
    replyChan chan bool
}

type readCounterRequest struct {
    replyChan chan int
}

func stateManager() {
    var st state
    requestChan := make(chan interface{})

    go func() {
        for request := range requestChan {
            switch req := request.(type) {
            case *incrementRequest:
                st.counter++
                req.replyChan <- true
            case *readCounterRequest:
                req.replyChan <- st.counter
            }
        }
    }()

    return requestChan
}

func incrementCounter(requestChan chan interface{}) {
    replyChan := make(chan bool)
    requestChan <- &incrementRequest{replyChan: replyChan}
    <-replyChan
}

func readCounter(requestChan chan interface{}) int {
    replyChan := make(chan int)
    requestChan <- &readCounterRequest{replyChan: replyChan}
    return <-replyChan
}
```

In this example, we have defined a simple state consisting of a
single counter. The stateManager function creates and returns a
requestChan, which is used by other goroutines to send requests to
the state manager.   The incrementCounter and readCounter
functions demonstrate how to interact with the state manager by

sending increment and read requests, respectively. The state manager goroutine uses a type switch to determine the type of each request and respond appropriately.

Advantages of this Pattern

- Race conditions are effectively avoided since the state is only accessed by a single goroutine.

- This pattern simplifies the handling of concurrent read and write operations on shared state.

- It aligns well with Go's philosophy of using channels to communicate between goroutines.

Considerations

- While this pattern effectively serializes access to the state and prevents race conditions, it can become a performance bottleneck if not designed carefully, particularly for high-frequency access patterns.

- The pattern requires careful design of request and response types to ensure flexibility and scalability of the state management logic.

Managing state with goroutines and channels is a powerful pattern in Go's concurrent programming toolkit. By encapsulating state within a single goroutine and serializing access through channels, developers can safely manage shared state without fearing the complexities associated with traditional lock-based concurrency mechanisms.

9.11   Pattern: Rate Limiting

Rate limiting is a crucial pattern in concurrent programming, especially when developing applications that interact with external resources or services, such as web APIs. It helps to prevent overwhelming a service with too many requests within a short timeframe, thus avoiding performance degradation or service unavailability. In the context of Go, implementing rate limiting can be achieved efficiently using channels and time.Tick function.

Let's explore how to implement a rate limiter in Go. The core idea is to use a ticker, which will release tokens into a channel at a specified interval. A token is simply a signal that allows a goroutine to proceed with its operation. This mechanism ensures that operations do not exceed a defined rate.

```go
package main

import (
    "fmt"
    "time"
)

func main() {
    requests := make(chan int, 5)
    for i := 1; i <= 5; i++ {
        requests <- i
    }
    close(requests)

    limiter := time.Tick(200 * time.Millisecond)

    for req := range requests {
        <-limiter
        fmt.Println("request", req, time.Now())
    }
}
```

In the above example, we create a channel `requests` to simulate incoming requests. We then use `time.Tick` to create a `limiter` channel that receives a value every 200 milliseconds. For each request, the program blocks on `<-limiter` until it can receive a value from the `limiter` channel, effectively throttling the processing to not exceed five requests per second.

For scenarios requiring more dynamic control over the rate of operations, the `time.Ticker` type can be used. Unlike `time.Tick`, which produces a fixed-rate ticker, `time.Ticker` provides more flexibility as it can be stopped and adjusted as needed.

```go
ticker := time.NewTicker(1 * time.Second)
```

```
2   defer ticker.Stop()
3
4   for {
5       select {
6       case <-ticker.C:
7           // Execute the operation
8       case <-someOtherChannel:
9           // Handle another case
10      }
11  }
```

In this pattern, it's also possible to implement a bursty rate limiter, which allows for short bursts of requests in addition to a steady rate limit. This is useful in scenarios where occasional spikes in demand need to be accommodated without fundamentally changing the overall rate limit.

```
1   burstyLimiter := make(chan time.Time, 3)
2
3   for i := 0; i < 3; i++ {
4       burstyLimiter <- time.Now()
5   }
6
7   go func() {
8       for t := range time.Tick(200 * time.Millisecond) {
9           burstyLimiter <- t
10      }
11  }()
12
13  for req := range requests {
14      <-burstyLimiter
15      fmt.Println("request", req, time.Now())
16  }
```

In the bursty limiter example, `burstyLimiter` is initialized with a capacity of 3, allowing it to immediately process three requests. It then continues at a fixed rate of 200 milliseconds per request. This approach effectively combines a burst capability with a steady rate limit, giving developers the flexibility to handle varying load patterns.

Understanding and implementing rate limiting in Go provides developers with a powerful tool for managing resource utilization, ensuring application stability, and preventing service degradation. By leveraging channels and ticker functions, Go makes it straightforward to incorporate rate limiting into concurrent applications, helping developers build more resilient and reliable systems.

9.12 Adapting Design Patterns for Concurrency

In the development lifecycle of software, especially within the context of concurrent programming in Go, adapting traditional design patterns to fit the model of concurrency can significantly enhance the performance, scalability, and maintainability of applications. This discussion will delve into how conventional design patterns can be refit or evolved to work effectively within a concurrent programming landscape, emphasizing patterns such as Singleton, Observer, and Command patterns, among others.

The Singleton Pattern: Traditionally, the Singleton pattern ensures that a class has only one instance and provides a global point of access to it. When adapting the Singleton pattern to a concurrent environment in Go, synchronization becomes critically significant to prevent multiple goroutines from creating singleton objects simultaneously.

```
package singleton

import (
    "sync"
)

type singleton struct{}

var (
    instance *singleton
    once sync.Once
)

func GetInstance() *singleton {
    once.Do(func() {
        instance = &singleton{}
    })
    return instance
}
```

The Observer Pattern: The Observer pattern suits scenarios where an object, termed as the subject, needs to automatically inform a list of objects, termed as observers, about state changes or events. This pattern can be adapted for concurrency by leveraging Go channels, thereby enabling the subject to broadcast events without being aware of the observers' identities, fostering a decoupled system architecture.

```go
package observer

type Subject struct {
    observers chan Observer
}

func NewSubject() *Subject {
    return &Subject{
        observers: make(chan Observer, 100),
    }
}

func (s *Subject) Subscribe(observer Observer) {
    s.observers <- observer
}

func (s *Subject) Notify(event interface{}) {
    go func() {
        for obs := range s.observers {
            obs.OnNotify(event)
        }
    }()
}
```

The Command Pattern: In its classic form, the Command pattern encapsulates a request as an object, thereby allowing for parameterization of clients with queues, requests, and operations. Adapting it for concurrency involves structuring the command execution to work through goroutines and channels, ensuring that commands can be executed asynchronously without blocking the main thread of execution.

```go
package command

import "fmt"

type Command interface {
    Execute()
}

type ConcreteCommand struct {
    Payload string
}
```

```
13  func (c *ConcreteCommand) Execute() {
14      fmt.Println("Executing command with payload:", c.Payload)
15  }
16
17  func ExecuteCommand(command Command) {
18      go command.Execute()
19  }
```

Adapting traditional design patterns for concurrency in Go not only involves syntactic changes but also a rethink in design philosophy. The essence lies in embracing Go's inherent features - goroutines and channels - to promote safe and efficient parallel execution. It is important to note, however, that though concurrency can boost an application's performance, it introduces complexity. Thus, the decision to adapt and use a particular design pattern in a concurrent manner should hinge upon a tangible benefit versus the additional complexity trade-off.

In summary, the transition or adaptation of design patterns to support concurrency is a non-trivial endeavor that requires a deep understanding of both the patterns in question and Go's concurrency model. It represents an advanced level of software design sophistication, which when done correctly, can lead to highly efficient and scalable concurrent applications.

9.13 Conclusion: Choosing the Right Pattern

Choosing the right concurrent design pattern in Go is pivotal for achieving optimal performance and maintainability in your applications. Each pattern discussed in this chapter offers unique advantages that can cater to specific scenarios in concurrent programming.

- The Worker Pool pattern is ideal for distributing tasks among a set of workers to parallelize workload. It efficiently manages multiple tasks that are independent of each other, thereby maximizing resource utilization and throughput. Employ this pattern when you have a significant volume of tasks that can be executed in parallel without interdependence.

269

- The `Pipeline` pattern is suitable for processing streams of data where each stage can process data concurrently before passing it to the next stage. This pattern facilitates the division of data processing into distinct steps, each of which can be optimized independently. Use the pipeline pattern for operations that require sequential processing where each step can start processing as soon as its input is available.

- `Fan-in` and `Fan-out` patterns are effective in scenarios where tasks need to operate on the same data in parallel (`Fan-out`) or when multiple data streams converge into a single processing unit (`Fan-in`). These patterns are particularly useful for workload distribution and aggregation in systems handling large datasets or requiring comprehensive data analysis.

- The `Publish/Subscribe` pattern enables loose coupling between components, where publishers and subscribers remain unaware of each other. This pattern excels in event-driven architectures and applications that need to distribute notifications or updates to multiple listeners efficiently.

- The `Future and Promise` pattern is designed to handle asynchronous operations, allowing a function to return immediately with a promise of future data. It is most beneficial in scenarios involving non-blocking operations or when coordinating multiple asynchronous tasks.

- In a concurrent environment, the `Singleton` pattern ensures that a class has only one instance and provides a global point of access to it. This pattern is useful when managing access to a resource that is shared across the entire application, ensuring consistency and avoiding resource contention.

- Error handling in concurrent patterns requires careful consideration. It is critical to design your system to gracefully handle failures without compromising the integrity or performance of the application. Techniques such as error propagation and recovery strategies should be employed based on the operational requirements of your application.

- For applications that need to balance workloads dynamically or manage state across multiple goroutines, patterns like Load Balancing with Go Channels and Managing State with Goroutines provide structured approaches to achieve these goals effectively.

- Lastly, the Rate Limiting pattern is invaluable for controlling the flow of operations, ensuring that your application does not overwhelm resources or exceed rate limits imposed by external systems or APIs.

In selecting the appropriate pattern, consider factors such as the nature of the task, data volume, dependency between tasks, performance requirements, and scalability needs. The choice of pattern not only affects the concurrency model but also the complexity and ease of understanding of your code. Therefore, evaluating the trade-offs associated with each pattern is crucial to designing efficient, robust, and maintainable concurrent applications in Go.

Remember, the patterns outlined in this chapter are not mutually exclusive and can be combined in various ways to address complex scenarios. Experimentation and experience will guide you in integrating these patterns seamlessly into your Go applications, harnessing the power of concurrency to build sophisticated, high-performance software.

Chapter 10

Concurrency Safety and Best Practices

Ensuring concurrency safety is paramount in the development of correct and reliable concurrent applications. This chapter addresses the crucial aspects of concurrency safety in Go, detailing strategies to avoid common issues such as race conditions, deadlocks, and other synchronization problems. It also compiles best practices for writing concurrent code, emphasizing patterns and techniques that enhance data integrity and prevent concurrent executions from interfering with each other. By adhering to these guidelines and employing the tools Go provides for concurrency safety, developers can create more secure, efficient, and maintainable concurrent applications.

10.1 Understanding Concurrency Safety

Concurrency safety concerns the ability of an application to execute multiple operations in parallel in a manner that does not lead to erroneous behavior or compromise the integrity of data. In the Go programming language, concurrency is a first-class citizen, designed into the language to enable efficient parallel processing. However, the power of concurrency comes with the responsibility of ensuring that concurrent execution does not lead to race conditions, deadlocks, or data corruption.

In Go, concurrency is primarily achieved using goroutines and channels. Goroutines are lightweight threads managed by the Go runtime, and channels provide a way for goroutines to communicate with each other. Despite the ease of spinning up thousands of goroutines, developers must be vigilant in managing access to shared resources to ensure concurrency safety.

Race Conditions

Race conditions occur when two or more goroutines access the same resource, such as a variable, and at least one of the accesses is a write. This can lead to unpredictable outcomes, as the result depends on the non-deterministic ordering of goroutine execution.

```
1   var counter int
2
3   func Increment() {
4       counter++
5   }
6
7   func main() {
8       for i := 0; i < 1000; i++ {
9           go Increment()
10      }
11      time.Sleep(2 * time.Second)
12      fmt.Println("Counter value:", counter)
13  }
```

In the example above, the `Increment` function is called by 1000 goroutines. Without proper synchronization, running this program multiple times will likely result in different values of `counter`, demonstrating a race condition.

To detect race conditions in Go, the race detector can be used by passing the -race flag to the go command.

Mutexes for Synchronization

To ensure that only one goroutine accesses a shared resource at a time, Go provides synchronization primitives like mutexes. A *mutex* (mutual exclusion) locks access to a resource, allowing only one goroutine to access the resource until the mutex is unlocked.

```
1  var counter int
2  var lock sync.Mutex
3
4  func Increment() {
5      lock.Lock()
6      counter++
7      lock.Unlock()
8  }
9
10 func main() {
11     for i := 0; i < 1000; i++ {
12         go Increment()
13     }
14     time.Sleep(2 * time.Second)
15     fmt.Println("Counter value:", counter)
16 }
```

In this revised example, a sync.Mutex is used to ensure that increments to the counter variable are synchronized, thus preventing the race condition.

Atomic Operations

For certain types of operations, Go provides atomic functions in the sync/atomic package that make low-level synchronization tasks simpler and faster than mutexes.

```
1  var counter int64
2
3  func Increment() {
4      atomic.AddInt64(&counter, 1)
5  }
6
7  func main() {
8      for i := 0; i < 1000; i++ {
9          go Increment()
10     }
11     time.Sleep(2 * time.Second)
12     fmt.Println("Counter value:", atomic.LoadInt64(&counter))
13 }
```

Using `atomic.AddInt64`, the increment operation on `counter` is made atomic, ensuring that increments happen in a manner that prevents race conditions without the explicit locking and unlocking seen with mutexes.

Ensuring concurrency safety in Go requires a deep understanding of how goroutines interact with shared resources, as well as a familiarity with the tools and patterns Go provides to manage this interaction safely. Employing these strategies effectively allows developers to harness the power of concurrency in Go, building applications that are both efficient and correct.

10.2　Identifying　and　Avoiding　Race Conditions

Race conditions occur in concurrent programming when two or more goroutines access shared data and try to change it at the same time. The outcome of this situation depends on the non-deterministic ordering of the goroutines' execution. To ensure concurrency safety, identifying and avoiding race conditions is imperative. This section will discuss various strategies for detecting race conditions in Go programs and methods to avert them effectively.

Understanding Race Conditions in Go

In Go, a race condition can compromise the integrity of data. It emerges when two or more goroutines access a shared variable concurrently, and at least one of the accesses is a write. This disorder in execution order can lead to unpredictable results, making the program behave incorrectly.

Using the Go Race Detector

The Go runtime includes a race detector tool, invoked by adding the -race flag when running or testing a program. This tool is instrumental in identifying race conditions by monitoring the program's execution and reporting detected races.

Example of using the race detector:

```
go run -race myprogram.go
```

If the race detector identifies a race condition, it outputs detailed information about the goroutines involved and the variables they access, as shown below:

```
==================
WARNING: DATA RACE
Read at 0x00c000014108 by goroutine 8:
  runtime.convT2E()
  myprogram.go:23 +0x3a

Previous write at 0x00c000014108 by goroutine 7:
  myprogram.go:16 +0x4b

Goroutine 8 (running) created at:
  myprogram.go:22 +0x67
Goroutine 7 (finished) created at:
  myprogram.go:15 +0x58
==================
```

Synchronization Techniques

To avoid race conditions, synchronization mechanisms can be used to coordinate access to shared resources. Mutexes (Mutual Exclusion Locks) are one such mechanism provided by Go's sync package.

Example of using a mutex to protect a shared variable:

```
var mu sync.Mutex
var counter int

func Increment() {
    mu.Lock()
    counter++
    mu.Unlock()
}
```

In the above example, `mu.Lock()` and `mu.Unlock()` ensure that only one goroutine can modify the `counter` variable at a time, thus preventing a race condition.

Design Patterns to Prevent Race Conditions

Proper design and architecture can significantly reduce the likelihood of introducing race conditions. Some effective patterns include:

- Encapsulating shared resources in a struct along with a mutex to protect access to the data.

- Using channels to synchronize and communicate between goroutines, following the principle of "Do not communicate by sharing memory; instead, share memory by communicating."

- Designing the application in a way that minimizes shared state or eliminates it entirely.

Identifying and avoiding race conditions early in the development process is crucial for building reliable and maintainable concurrent applications in Go. Employing the Go race detector, utilizing synchronization techniques like mutexes, and following sound design principles can help achieve concurrency safety and prevent data corruption.

10.3   Effective Use of Mutexes for Data Protection

In concurrent programming, protecting shared resources from simultaneous access by multiple goroutines is essential to ensure data integrity. Go provides a synchronization primitive called a mutex, an abbreviation for mutual exclusion, to handle such scenarios. The 'sync' package in Go includes the 'Mutex' type, which allows developers to create critical sections of code that only one goroutine can enter at a time.

Basics of Mutex Usage

To demonstrate the basic usage of mutexes, consider the following example:

```
1   package main
2
3   import (
4       "fmt"
5       "sync"
6   )
7
8   var (
9       counter int
10      lock sync.Mutex
11  )
12
13  func increment() {
14      lock.Lock()
15      defer lock.Unlock()
16      counter++
17  }
18
19  func main() {
20      var wg sync.WaitGroup
21      for i := 0; i < 1000; i++ {
22          wg.Add(1)
23          go func() {
24              increment()
25              wg.Done()
26          }()
27      }
28      wg.Wait()
29      fmt.Println("Final counter value:", counter)
30  }
```

In this example, the 'increment' function uses 'lock.Lock()' to acquire the mutex before incrementing the 'counter' variable and 'defer lock.Unlock()' to ensure the mutex is released after incrementing, regardless of how the function exits. This ensures that only one goroutine can modify 'counter' at any time, preventing data races.

Avoiding Deadlocks

While mutexes are powerful for protecting shared resources, incorrect usage can lead to deadlocks, where goroutines are permanently blocked, waiting to acquire a mutex held by another goroutine. To avoid deadlocks:

- Acquire mutex locks in a consistent order across different goroutines.

- Prefer smaller critical sections to reduce the time a mutex is held.

- Use 'defer' to unlock immediately after locking to ensure mutexes are always released, even if a panic occurs.

Careful management of mutexes is crucial for deadlock prevention. Consider the structure and flow of your program to ensure that locks are acquired and released in a way that does not lead to circular dependencies between goroutines.

Performance Considerations

While mutexes are necessary for ensuring data integrity in concurrent programs, overusing them can lead to performance bottlenecks. To mitigate this:

- Minimize the amount of work done inside critical sections.

- Use more granular locks for different parts of the data, if possible, to allow more concurrent access.

- Consider alternative synchronization techniques or data structures, such as atomic operations or channels, for specific use cases where they may offer better performance.

It is also valuable to profile your application to identify and address mutex-related performance issues. Tools like Go's built-in pprof can help identify contention points in concurrent programs.

Mutexes are a vital tool for managing data integrity in concurrent programming in Go. Correctly using mutexes to protect shared resources from concurrent access ensures that your applications are both correct and efficient. By following best practices for mutex usage, including avoiding deadlocks and being mindful of performance implications, you can effectively use mutexes to safeguard critical sections of your concurrent Go programs.

10.4 Deadlock Prevention Techniques

Deadlocks in concurrent programming are problematic scenarios where two or more processes hold resources and wait for the other to release their resources, leading to a situation where none of the processes can proceed. Preventing deadlocks is essential for ensuring that applications run smoothly without halt. This section highlights techniques to avoid deadlocks, ensuring that your Go applications remain responsive and efficient.

Resource Allocation Order

One effective strategy to prevent deadlocks is to enforce a global order in which resources are requested. By ensuring that all goroutines acquire resources in a pre-defined sequence, it becomes impossible for a circular wait condition—one of the necessary conditions for a deadlock—to occur.

```
1  func requestResources() {
2      // Assuming Resource1 and Resource2 need to be acquired
3      // Always acquire Resource1 before Resource2
4      lockResource1()
5      lockResource2()
6      // Perform operations
7      unlockResource2()
8      unlockResource1()
9  }
```

It is crucial that the same order is preserved across the entire application to avoid deadlocks effectively.

Using Timeouts

Another technique is to implement timeouts when waiting for resources.   This method prevents a goroutine from waiting indefinitely for a resource that might be held by another process. The Go programming language provides functionalities such as select with time.After for implementing timeouts.

```
1   select {
2   case <-lockChannel:
3       // Acquired the lock
4   case <-time.After(10 * time.Second):
5       // Timeout occurred
6       return errors.New("timeout while trying to acquire lock")
7   }
```

This approach ensures that the program remains responsive, allowing it to handle deadlock scenarios gracefully by either retrying the operation or aborting it.

Avoid Holding Multiple Locks Simultaneously

Whenever possible, design your application logic to reduce the necessity of a goroutine holding multiple locks at the same time. If this is unavoidable, ensure that all goroutines acquire and release the locks in the same order.

Deadlock Detection Tools

Leveraging deadlock detection tools can also aid in identifying and rectifying deadlocks during the development phase. Go provides the go-deadlock tool as part of its toolchain, which can replace the standard sync package mutexes to detect potential deadlocks in your code.

```
Potential deadlock detected:
[P1] holds [R1] and waits for [R2]
[P2] holds [R2] and waits for [R1]
```

By analyzing the output provided by such tools, developers can pinpoint the exact location and condition that might cause a deadlock.

Testing with Goroutines

To ensure that your application is free from deadlocks, extensive testing with multiple goroutines is necessary. Simulating parallel execution paths that interact with shared resources can help uncover deadlocks that might not be evident during the regular execution flow.

```
1  go func() {
2      lockResource1()
3      lockResource2()
4      unlockResource2()
5      unlockResource1()
6  }()
7  go func() {
8      lockResource2()
9      lockResource1()
10     unlockResource1()
11     unlockResource2()
12 }()
13 // Wait for goroutines to finish
```

Routine code reviews and employing these deadlock prevention techniques can significantly reduce the likelihood of encountering deadlocks in production. Implementing a combination of these strategies will create a robust foundation for writing concurrent programs in Go.

10.5   Writing Thread-Safe Data Structures

Concurrency safety in Go is a key concern when it comes to designing and implementing data structures. Thread-safe data structures are designed to guarantee that they operate correctly in a concurrent environment, where multiple goroutines access and modify data simultaneously. The design of thread-safe data structures revolves around ensuring that concurrent access does not lead to race conditions, data corruption, or any other form of undefined behavior.

In the development of thread-safe data structures, synchronization primitives such as mutexes and channels are fundamental. These primitives are used to serialize access to data, ensuring that only one goroutine can access critical sections of code at a time. This section elaborates on strategies and patterns for implementing thread-safe data structures in Go.

Effective Use of Mutexes for Data Protection

Mutexes are one of the most direct tools to safeguard data structures in concurrent programming. The sync.Mutex and sync.RWMutex types from the Go standard library provide exclusive and reader/writer locks, respectively. When wrapping a data structure with a mutex, it is vital to ensure that all accesses, both reads and writes, are performed with the mutex locked. Here's an example implementation of a thread-safe counter using a mutex:

```
type SafeCounter struct {
    mu sync.Mutex
    value int
}

func (c *SafeCounter) Increment() {
    c.mu.Lock()
    c.value++
    c.mu.Unlock()
}

func (c *SafeCounter) Value() int {
    c.mu.Lock()
    defer c.mu.Unlock()
    return c.value
}
```

In this example, both Increment and Value methods lock the mutex to ensure that read and write operations are not concurrently executed, thus maintaining the data integrity of value.

Leveraging Channels for Safe Data Exchange

Channels in Go not only facilitate communication between goroutines but can also ensure thread-safety by controlling access to data. By making the data structure's critical section only accessible via channel operations, developers can avoid explicit locking and unlocking as seen with mutexes. Following is an illustration of using channels to implement a thread-safe queue:

```go
type SafeQueue struct {
    enqueueChan chan interface{}
    dequeueChan chan interface{}
}

func NewSafeQueue() *SafeQueue {
    q := &SafeQueue{
        enqueueChan: make(chan interface{}, 1),
        dequeueChan: make(chan interface{}, 1),
    }
    go q.start()
    return q
}

func (q *SafeQueue) start() {
    var queue []interface{}
    for {
        if len(queue) == 0 {
            elem := <-q.enqueueChan
            queue = append(queue, elem)
        } else {
            select {
            case elem := <-q.enqueueChan:
                queue = append(queue, elem)
            case q.dequeueChan <- queue[0]:
                queue = queue[1:]
            }
        }
    }
}
```

In this approach, the start method runs in its goroutine and manages the queue's state, ensuring that enqueue and dequeue operations are inherently thread-safe. Data is exchanged via enqueueChan and dequeueChan, without the need for explicit locking mechanisms.

Immutable Data Structures

Another strategy for achieving thread safety is the use of immutable data structures. By definition, an immutable data structure cannot be altered after it is created. Hence, concurrent access to such structures does not pose a threat to data integrity. While immutable data structures may seem restrictive, they simplify reasoning about code and can significantly reduce the complexity associated with synchronization.

A simplistic immutable stack implementation could look like this:

```
type ImmutableStack struct {
    head interface{}
    tail *ImmutableStack
}

func NewImmutableStack() *ImmutableStack {
    return &ImmutableStack{}
}

func (s *ImmutableStack) Push(v interface{}) *ImmutableStack {
    return &ImmutableStack{head: v, tail: s}
}

func (s *ImmutableStack) Pop() (*ImmutableStack, interface{}) {
    if s.tail == nil {
        return nil, nil // Empty stack
    }
    return s.tail, s.head
}
```

This implementation ensures thread safety by returning a new stack instance upon each mutation, avoiding any race conditions associated with concurrent modifications.

By understanding and applying these strategies, developers can effectively design and implement thread-safe data structures in Go. These principles form the foundation for building reliable and concurrent applications, maximizing data integrity, and minimizing the risks associated with concurrent modifications.

10.6   Best Practices for Using Channels

Channels in Go are powerful tools for managing concurrency. They allow threads or goroutines to communicate with each other to prevent data races and ensure synchronization. However, improper usage can lead to deadlocks, goroutine leaks, or inefficient resource utilization. In this section, we will discuss the best practices for using channels effectively.

Choosing the Right Channel Type

Go offers two types of channels: unbuffered and buffered. The choice between them impacts the program's synchronization characteristics and performance.

- **Unbuffered channels** guarantee that a send operation will block until another goroutine performs a receive operation, ensuring perfect synchronization. This is suitable for ensuring that a task is taken up immediately as it is sent.

- **Buffered channels** provide a buffer, allowing sends to proceed even if the receive is not immediate, given the buffer is not full. This can improve performance by reducing delays between goroutines but requires careful sizing to avoid underutilization or overbuffering which leads to high memory consumption.

Initialization of Channels

Channels must be initialized before use. A nil channel blocks forever both on send and receive operations, making it useful for disabling a channel operation dynamically. However, improperly initialized channels can cause goroutine leaks. Always initialize channels with the built-in make function.

```
1  ch := make(chan int) // unbuffered channel
2  bufCh := make(chan int, 10) // buffered channel with size 10
```

Closing Channels Carefully

A sender may close a channel to indicate that no more values will be sent. Receivers can use a two-value assignment to check whether a channel is closed.

```
1  v, ok := <-ch
2  if !ok {
3      // handle channel closed
4  }
```

However, only the sender should close a channel, and never the receiver. Closing a channel from multiple goroutines can lead to panics. Moreover, sending on a closed channel also causes a panic. Thus, care must be taken to ensure channels are closed precisely once and only by the sender.

Select Statements for Channel Operations

The select statement allows a goroutine to wait on multiple communication operations. It picks one at random if multiple channels are ready.

```
select {
case msg1 := <-ch1:
    fmt.Println("Received", msg1)
case msg2 := <-ch2:
    fmt.Println("Received", msg2)
default:
    fmt.Println("No messages")
}
```

Using the default case ensures non-blocking operations, which is useful for combining channel operations with other work. However, using it improperly can lead to busy waiting, wasting CPU resources.

Avoiding Goroutine Leaks

Goroutine leaks occur when a goroutine is blocked forever, unable to proceed. To prevent this, always ensure that every send operation has a corresponding receive operation. Additionally, consider using context cancellation or select with a timeout to terminate goroutines that wait too long.

```
ctx, cancel := context.WithTimeout(context.Background(), 100*time.Millisecond)
defer cancel()

select {
case <-ctx.Done():
    fmt.Println("Operation timed out")
case <-ch:
    // proceed with normal operation
}
```

Channel Capacity and Performance

The capacity of buffered channels significantly impacts performance. Insufficient capacity can cause frequent blocking, reducing concurrency. Conversely, excessive capacity might increase memory footprint without tangible benefits. Profile your application to find the optimal buffer size, considering throughput, latency, and memory consumption.

In summary, channels are indispensable for concurrent programming in Go, but they require careful management. Adhering to these best practices can prevent common concurrency issues, thereby achieving more predictable and efficient execution of concurrent operations.

10.7 Safe Shutdown Patterns for Goroutines

Ensuring the graceful shutdown of goroutines is an essential aspect of writing robust, concurrent applications in Go. A safe shutdown process guarantees that goroutines terminate correctly, resources are released, and data integrity is preserved. This section will explore strategies to implement such patterns effectively.

Utilizing the Context Package

The context package in Go is designed to enable cancellation signals across API boundaries and goroutines. It offers a standardized way to stop processes and cleanup resources gracefully.

```
import (
    "context"
    "fmt"
    "time"
)

func worker(ctx context.Context) {
    for {
        select {
        case <-ctx.Done():
            fmt.Println("Worker shutting down")
```

```
12          return
13       default:
14          fmt.Println("Worker doing work")
15          time.Sleep(1 * time.Second)
16       }
17    }
18 }
19
20 func main() {
21    ctx, cancel := context.WithCancel(context.Background())
22    go worker(ctx)
23
24    time.Sleep(5 * time.Second)
25    cancel() // sends a cancellation signal
26    time.Sleep(1 * time.Second) // give goroutine time to shut down
27 }
```

In the example above, the worker goroutine operates in a loop, periodically checking for a cancellation signal via ctx.Done() channel. Upon receiving a cancellation signal, it performs the necessary shutdown procedures and exits.

WaitGroup for Synchronized Shutdown

sync.WaitGroup is useful for waiting for a collection of goroutines to finish executing before proceeding. This can be beneficial when you have multiple concurrent operations that must all complete before your program exits.

```
1  import (
2     "fmt"
3     "sync"
4     "time"
5  )
6
7  func worker(id int, wg *sync.WaitGroup) {
8     defer wg.Done()
9
10    fmt.Printf("Worker %d starting\n", id)
11    time.Sleep(2 * time.Second)
12    fmt.Printf("Worker %d done\n", id)
13 }
14
15 func main() {
16    var wg sync.WaitGroup
17
18    for i := 1; i <= 5; i++ {
19       wg.Add(1)
20       go worker(i, &wg)
```

```
21        }
22
23        wg.Wait() // Wait for all workers to complete
24        fmt.Println("All workers completed")
25   }
```

In this example, main will not proceed past wg.Wait() until all goroutines have called wg.Done(), ensuring a synchronized shutdown.

Combining Context and WaitGroup

For a comprehensive solution, combining context for cancellation signaling with sync.WaitGroup for synchronization can handle more complex shutdown scenarios.

```
1   func main() {
2       ctx, cancel := context.WithCancel(context.Background())
3       var wg sync.WaitGroup
4
5       for i := 1; i <= 5; i++ {
6           wg.Add(1)
7           go func(id int) {
8               defer wg.Done()
9               worker(ctx, id)
10          }(i)
11      }
12
13      time.Sleep(5 * time.Second) // simulate work
14      cancel() // Send cancellation signal
15      wg.Wait() // Wait for all workers to exit gracefully
16      fmt.Println("All workers shutdown cleanly")
17  }
```

This pattern provides the flexibility to cancel operations mid-way and still wait for the clean shutdown of all goroutines, ensuring resources are not leaked, and the application exits as intended.

10.8 Error Handling in Concurrent Applications

Error handling in concurrent applications presents unique challenges due to the non-sequential execution of concurrent

processes.   Effective error handling strategies are essential for
maintaining the reliability and robustness of applications.   This
section discusses methods to handle errors gracefully in a
concurrent programming environment using Go.

The basic principle of error handling in Go is straightforward - errors
are values that can be returned and handled explicitly. This principle holds true in concurrent programming as well, but with added
complexity due to the concurrent execution of goroutines.

Using Channels for Error Propagation

One common pattern for error handling in concurrent Go programs
involves using channels to propagate errors from goroutines back to
the main or parent goroutine.

```
 1  func worker(input <-chan int, output chan<- int, errChan chan<- error) {
 2      for n := range input {
 3          if n < 0 {
 4              errChan <- fmt.Errorf("negative number not allowed: %v", n)
 5              return
 6          }
 7          // Simulate work
 8          time.Sleep(time.Second)
 9          output <- n * 2
10      }
11  }
```

In this example, a worker goroutine performs operations on numbers
it receives. If it encounters a negative number, it sends an error on
the errChan channel and terminates.

Handling Errors in Select Statements

When using channels for communication among goroutines, select
statements become an essential construct for non-blocking channel
operations. They can also be utilized to elegantly handle errors in
conjunction with normal data flow.

```
 1  select {
 2  case n := <-output:
 3      fmt.Println("Processed number:", n)
 4  case err := <-errChan:
```

```
5      log.Println("Error received:", err)
6    }
```

This `select` statement waits on multiple channel operations. If an error is sent on the errChan, it gets handled immediately, preventing it from silently passing through the system.

Error Aggregation in Concurrent Workflows

In scenarios involving numerous concurrent operations, it's often necessary to aggregate errors for collective handling post-execution. A common approach is to use a synchronized data structure or a dedicated error handling goroutine to collect and aggregate errors.

```
1    var wg sync.WaitGroup
2    errChan := make(chan error, 100) // Buffered channel
3
4    for _, task := range tasks {
5        wg.Add(1)
6        go func(task Task) {
7            defer wg.Done()
8            if err := task.Do(); err != nil {
9                errChan <- err
10           }
11       }(task)
12   }
13
14   go func() {
15       wg.Wait()
16       close(errChan)
17   }()
18
19   var errors []error
20   for err := range errChan {
21       errors = append(errors, err)
22   }
23
24   if len(errors) > 0 {
25       for _, err := range errors {
26           log.Println("Task error:", err)
27       }
28   }
```

This method uses a WaitGroup to wait for all tasks to complete and a buffered error channel to collect errors concurrently. After all tasks are done, errors are aggregated from the channel for further handling.

Best Practices

When handling errors in concurrent applications, consider the following best practices:

- Use buffered channels for error propagation to prevent goroutines from getting blocked on channel sends.

- Aggregate errors for batch processing when dealing with multiple concurrent operations.

- Ensure proper error logging and use structured logging for better error traceability.

- Consider context cancellation to stop goroutines gracefully in case of errors.

Effective error handling in concurrent Go applications requires a combination of idiomatic Go error handling techniques and concurrency-specific strategies. By leveraging channels for error propagation, employing select statements for handling errors alongside regular operations, aggregating errors from multiple sources, and adhering to best practices, developers can ensure that their concurrent applications are both robust and reliable.

10.9   Testing for Concurrency Issues

Testing for concurrency issues is an essential step in ensuring the reliability and correctness of concurrent applications. Due to the inherent complexity and non-deterministic nature of concurrent executions, traditional testing methods may not suffice. This section will explore effective strategies and tools for detecting and diagnosing concurrency issues in Go programs, such as race conditions, deadlocks, and other synchronization problems.

The first tool in our arsenal is the Go Race Detector. The Race Detector is a powerful tool that helps identify race conditions in a program. A race condition occurs when two or more threads access shared data concurrently, and at least one thread modifies the data without proper synchronization, leading to unpredictable results. To use the Race Detector, compile and run your Go program with the -race flag. For instance:

```
go run -race myprogram.go
```

When a race condition is detected, the Race Detector will output detailed information about the race, including the involved goroutines and the shared variables. Here's an example of the output:

```
==================
WARNING: DATA RACE
Read by goroutine 8:
  runtime.convT2E()
    /usr/local/go/src/runtime/iface.go:128 +0x0
  main.main.func1()
    /home/user/myprogram.go:25 +0x3e

Previous write by goroutine 7:
  main.main()
    /home/user/myprogram.go:23 +0x2f
==================
```

This output precisely pinpoints the lines of code involved in the race, facilitating debugging efforts.

Next, let's discuss deadlock detection. Deadlocks occur when two or more goroutines are waiting on each other to release a resource they need, causing the program to hang indefinitely. Go's runtime has some built-in tools to detect potential deadlocks. When the Go runtime detects that all goroutines are asleep and there is no possibility of awakening them, it will panic, indicating a deadlock situation. However, this detection is limited and may not catch more complex deadlocks that involve channel operations or non-Goroutine-blocking operations.

To augment the Go runtime's capabilities, developers can use static analysis tools such as go-deadlock or deadcode to identify potential deadlocks or unreachable code that could hint at synchronization issues.

For a comprehensive testing strategy, it's also essential to incorporate unit tests that simulate concurrent access to shared resources. Here, table-driven tests in Go can be particularly useful. They allow you to define multiple test cases (including those meant to stress concurrency primitives) and run them systematically. Using sync.WaitGroup or channels can help coordinate goroutines within tests to simulate complex concurrent interactions.

Lastly, consider employing fuzz testing for concurrent applications. Fuzz testing involves generating random inputs to explore the program's execution paths and can be especially effective in uncovering rare, hidden concurrency issues that would be difficult to detect otherwise.

Testing for concurrency issues requires a multifaceted approach that combines dynamic analysis, static analysis, unit testing, and fuzz testing. Developers should leverage the Go Race Detector and pay attention to the runtime's deadlock detection messages during development. Additionally, employing static analysis tools and adopting comprehensive testing strategies will help ensure that your concurrent Go applications are robust, reliable, and free of concurrency-related bugs.

10.10   Performance   Considerations   in Concurrent Programs

In this section, we will discuss the critical aspects of performance in concurrent programs, focusing on Go. Writing concurrent programs brings a unique set of challenges, particularly regarding performance. The promise of concurrency is to run parts of your program in parallel, potentially leveraging multiple cores to achieve faster execution times. However, if not carefully managed, concurrent programs can suffer from various performance issues, leading to slower execution times than their sequential counterparts.

First, let's consider the overhead associated with creating and managing goroutines. Goroutines are lightweight when compared to threads in other programming languages, but they are not free.

The Go runtime has to manage the goroutines, including scheduling and switching between them. This overhead increases with the number of goroutines, especially when the number far exceeds the number of available CPU cores.

```
1  go func() {
2      // Example goroutine
3  }()
```

To measure the impact of goroutine overhead on performance, developers can use benchmarking tools provided by Go, such as 'testing.B'. It's essential to compare the performance of concurrent code with its sequential counterpart to ensure that concurrency is providing the intended benefits.

```
BenchmarkConcurrentFunction-8    1000000    1234 ns/op
BenchmarkSequentialFunction-8    2000000     567 ns/op
```

Another area of concern is the misuse of synchronization primitives such as mutexes. While mutexes are necessary for avoiding race conditions, excessive locking can lead to performance bottlenecks. When multiple goroutines contend for the same lock, they are serialized, negating the benefits of running concurrently.

```
1  var mu sync.Mutex
2
3  mu.Lock()
4  // Critical section
5  mu.Unlock()
```

To mitigate this, developers can use more granular locking or other synchronization primitives like channels, which can offer better performance in some scenarios. Understanding the specific requirements and behavior of the concurrent program is crucial to choosing the appropriate synchronization mechanism.

- Use sync.Mutex judiciously to avoid extensive blocking.

- Consider using buffered channels to reduce the need for locks.

- Employ sync.Pool to reuse objects and reduce garbage collection overhead.

Further, it's important to understand the cost of communication between goroutines, particularly when using channels. While channels provide a convenient and safe way to transfer data between goroutines, they come with overhead, especially unbuffered channels that synchronize sender and receiver.

```
1  ch := make(chan int)
2
3  go func() {
4      ch <- 42 // Sending data to channel
5  }()
6
7  value := <- ch // Receiving data from channel
```

When performance is critical, the choice between unbuffered and buffered channels can significantly affect the application's throughput and latency.   Buffered channels should be used judiciously, as they introduce memory overhead but can reduce the frequency of synchronization, improving performance.

Finally, it's crucial to adopt a profiling-guided approach to optimizing concurrent programs. Go's toolchain includes powerful profiling tools that can help identify bottlenecks in CPU usage, memory allocations, and blocking operations. These tools can uncover subtle issues that are not apparent through code inspection or benchmarking alone.

- Use go tool pprof to profile CPU and memory usage.

- Employ trace tool for understanding goroutine scheduling and blocking.

- Optimize based on evidence gathered through profiling rather than intuition.

While concurrency has the potential to improve performance significantly, achieving this requires careful consideration of the overhead associated with concurrent constructs, prudent use of synchronization primitives, and a commitment to profiling and optimization. By adhering to these performance considerations, developers can harness the full power of concurrency in Go, creating efficient and scalable applications.

10.11 Avoiding   Common   Pitfalls   in Concurrent Programming

Ensuring the correctness of a concurrent program demands meticulous attention to common pitfalls that can easily disrupt the intended behavior of the software. This section discusses several widespread issues in concurrent programming within Go and provides actionable strategies to avoid them.

Neglecting to Handle Race Conditions

A fundamental issue in concurrent programming is the race condition, where the outcome of the program depends on the non-deterministic ordering of operations execution. This can lead to unpredictable behavior and data corruption.

```
1  func updateCounter(wg *sync.WaitGroup, m *sync.Mutex, counter *int) {
2      m.Lock()
3      *counter++
4      m.Unlock()
5      wg.Done()
6  }
```

The code snippet demonstrates a basic pattern for updating a shared counter variable in a race-condition-free manner by employing a sync.Mutex to ensure that only one goroutine can modify the counter at any given time.

Misusing Locks and Causing Deadlocks

Improper use of locks can lead to deadlocks, where two or more goroutines are waiting on each other to release locks, causing the program to freeze indefinitely.

A common deadlock scenario occurs when a goroutine acquires a lock and then, within the same scope, attempts to acquire it again before releasing it. Another scenario is when multiple goroutines acquire locks in an inconsistent order.

To prevent deadlocks, always acquire locks in a consistent order and consider using a `sync.RWMutex` when possible, which allows multiple readers but only a single writer, thus reducing the locking contention.

Overusing Goroutines

While goroutines are lightweight and efficient, spawning an excessive number of them without bounds can lead to performance issues, including high memory usage and potentially exhausting system resources.

To mitigate this, use buffered channels or a worker pool pattern to limit the number of goroutines that can be active at a given time.

```
1  func worker(id int, jobs <-chan int, results chan<- int) {
2      for j := range jobs {
3          results <- j * 2
4      }
5  }
```

This pattern allows for fine-grained control over the number of concurrent worker goroutines processing tasks, enhancing the scalability and responsiveness of the application.

Ignoring Goroutine Leaks

Goroutines, once started, continue execution until completion. A common pitfall is unintentionally forgetting about a goroutine, leading to a leak where the goroutine remains active in the background, consuming resources.

To avoid leaks, ensure all goroutines can exit, either by reaching the end of their function or through explicit cancellation signals via context cancellation or closing a channel.

```
1  ctx, cancel := context.WithCancel(context.Background())
2  go func() {
3      for {
4          select {
5          case <-ctx.Done():
6              return
```

```
 7        default:
 8            // Perform work...
 9        }
10    }
11 }()
12 // Cancel the goroutine when no longer needed
13 cancel()
```

This approach allows for the graceful termination of goroutines, preventing resource leaks and ensuring that system resources are efficiently utilized.

By being aware of these common pitfalls and employing the outlined strategies, developers can significantly enhance the robustness and reliability of their concurrent applications in Go, leading to software that is both performant and maintainable.

10.12 Concurrency Patterns for Scalability and Maintainability

Achieving scalability and maintainability in concurrent programming requires a structured approach to design and implementation. This section will discuss several concurrency patterns that are instrumental in building applications that are not only scalable but also easier to maintain. These patterns include the Worker Pool, Pipeline, Publish-Subscribe, and the Actor Model. By leveraging these patterns, developers can significantly reduce the complexity associated with concurrent programming, mitigate common concurrency issues, and enhance the performance of their applications.

Worker Pool

The Worker Pool pattern involves creating a set of worker goroutines to perform tasks concurrently. This pattern is particularly useful for limiting the number of goroutines that are active at any given time, thereby controlling resource utilization.

The main components of this pattern are a pool of worker goroutines, a task queue, and a dispatcher.

```go
package main

import (
    "fmt"
    "sync"
)

func worker(tasksChan <-chan int, wg *sync.WaitGroup) {
    for task := range tasksChan {
        fmt.Printf("Worker processing task: %d\n", task)
        wg.Done()
    }
}

func main() {
    var wg sync.WaitGroup
    tasks := []int{1, 2, 3, 4, 5}
    tasksChan := make(chan int, len(tasks))

    for i := 0; i < 3; i++ {
        go worker(tasksChan, &wg)
    }

    wg.Add(len(tasks))
    for _, task := range tasks {
        tasksChan <- task
    }
    close(tasksChan)

    wg.Wait()
}
```

This code demonstrates the Worker Pool pattern in Go, where tasks are distributed to a fixed number of goroutines. This technique helps in managing resource utilization efficiently while maintaining high concurrency levels.

Pipeline

The Pipeline pattern structures the processing steps of data as a sequence of operations, with each operation executed in its goroutine. Data flows from one stage to the next, enabling concurrent processing of different parts of the data. A critical aspect of this pattern is chaining channels to connect the output of one stage to the input of another.

```go
package main

import "fmt"

func generator(nums ...int) <-chan int {
    out := make(chan int)
    go func() {
        for _, n := range nums {
            out <- n
        }
        close(out)
    }()
    return out
}

func square(input <-chan int) <-chan int {
    out := make(chan int)
    go func() {
        for n := range input {
            out <- n * n
        }
        close(out)
    }()
    return out
}

func main() {
    gen := generator(2, 3)
    sq := square(gen)

    for result := range sq {
        fmt.Println(result)
    }
}
```

This code snippet illustrates a simple Pipeline pattern implementation in Go, where numbers are generated, squared, and then output in a manner that leverages concurrent execution.

Publish-Subscribe

In the Publish-Subscribe pattern, messages are broadcasted to multiple subscribers concurrently. This pattern decouples the message sender from its receivers, allowing messages to be processed by multiple subscribers in parallel without direct knowledge of each other.

Actor Model

The Actor Model abstracts concurrency control by treating "actors" as the fundamental unit of computation. Each actor can process messages, maintain state, and send messages to other actors. The Actor Model simplifies concurrency by ensuring that messages to any given actor are processed in sequence, thus avoiding race conditions by design.

Employing these concurrency patterns can significantly enhance the scalability and maintainability of applications. Each pattern offers a unique approach to structuring concurrent computations, and by understanding their strengths and use cases, developers can choose the most suitable pattern(s) for their specific needs.